ONE UNDER

Book II of the End of Tour Series

Pete Thron

ONE UNDER

Book II : End of Tour Series

Published in the United States of America

ISBN: 978-1-68564-414-7

The author and publisher shall have neither liability nor responsibility to any person or entity with respect to any loss or damage caused, or alleged to have been caused, directly or indirectly, by the information in this book. Names of confidential informants and some suspects have been changed.

Warning: This book contains graphic descriptions of crimes and adult language.

DEDICATION

This book is dedicated to my brother Phil, my sister Janice, and my wife Aidana.

Thank you all for always being there during the writing of this book.

You've been the glue that's kept me together.

ACKNOWLEDGEMENTS

Book cover designer Michael Corvin, and to Aidana and Allan for helping with me the idea for the book cover.

Lastly thank you to Ralph Friedman for writing the forward.

FORWARD

I read Pete Thorn's first book, End of Tour, a cautionary tale of the pitfalls of being a career law enforcement officer, a subject with which I am very familiar, and a fascinating story. It was indeed an honor to be asked to write the Forward to his second book, One Under, a continuation of Pete's riveting experiences dealing with his post-police experiences which resulted in him doing time in prison.

Pete's writing expertise is on full display in both books; One Under capturing the heart-wrenching circumstances of his incarceration and his ability to deal with it. This fast-paced story tells of conditions which landed him in prison and how he survived, no mean feat for a former law enforcement officer. I couldn't put it down. There's a lesson to be learned here, and you don't have to be "on the job" to realize the value and depth of Pete's harrowing experiences and the lessons learned. Everyone can benefit from this taut tale of survival, Pete's strength of mind and body and his will to survive.

Detective Ralph Friedman NYPD (ret.)

Co-author of Street Warrior: The True Story of the NYPD's most Decorated Detective and the Era that Created Him and subject of Street Justice: The Bronx television series.

SEPTEMBER 2020

CHAPTER ONE

The radio sounded off. "Any 25 units in the area for multiple shots fired in the vicinity of 135th street and Park Avenue?"

There were no NYPD or housing patrol cars available. It was a busy night, and every unit was out on a job. I responded to central.

"This is housing crime, put us responding."

"Okay, crime the perpetrator is a Hispanic male wearing a tan jacket."

"10-4 K." Rhino checked his Glock.

"Ready for action Batman."

As I rolled up to the area where the shots had been reported being fired, I heard two more bursts from a large caliber handgun. The reverberations imitated that of a cannon.

"That is not good brother, sounds like a.45 or.357 magnum." I killed the lights on our unmarked car and slowly pulled along the length of 134th street.

"Bat, when we exit the cruiser, keep close enough so that we have a visual of each other. Hand signals only brother." I gave him a thumbs up as a response.

"Rhino, no flashlights."

The building had a square light fixture on the wall near the roof, but it was old, causing it to blink on and off. The alleyway had hardly any light. "Rhino, I think we can navigate through the darkness without being seen. Go to hand signals now brother."

As we exited the unmarked, I caught a whiff of the fresh pinch of the Skoal chewing tobacco he had just put in his mouth. Damn, that crap was potent when he first put it in. He spit out a piece that clung to his lower lip. Smiling, he let out a big 'Oh, yeah Bat, that tastes like heaven'.

Every day he would pack a new tin, holding it in the palm of his hand while he snapped his fingers. His first finger would hit the side of the round canister. That provided him with a tight pack of moist chew.

"My brother, this is a nice blend today." He always extended a full hand of chew to me, adding, "Stop being a pussy and take a plug bro."

My answer was always the same. "No thank you, Rhino. Did anyone ever tell you that is such a freaking disgusting habit?"

"Yes, sir, all the time. Screw them, I love it. I never go in the field without my dip." If we were in the cruiser or drinking at a bar, he would spit it into an empty Styrofoam cup. It wasn't unlike him to chew that shit during the entire tour.

Sometimes he would even fill the cup up with tobacco juice and innocently ask, "Would you like a sip?"

I'd gag simply at the smell. "Get that crap away from me."

"You know one day you are going to mistakenly drink that instead of your coffee, Pete." We would laugh our asses off every time he said that to me.

"Let's go catch this fucker, Bat. Oh, by the way, I heard you were the second-best housing cop in the city."

"That's funny. I heard the same thing about you, Rhino. Brother, we will always be Second to None."

We were hand motioning to each other as we entered the poorly lit alleyway. The passage was in between two desolate buildings that looked like they would crumble if a hard wind blew through. The ground was littered with broken glass, bricks that had fallen from the buildings, and used heroin needles that still had dried blood inside them.

I spotted a dark figure about twenty feet away from me. The perp wheeled on me and fired three rounds into my chest and torso. It felt like the bullets were ripping through me like wildfire. I returned fire, squeezing off six rounds. Not one of my shots hit their mark.

"What the fuck! They should've stopped him dead in his tracks. He should be down for the count by now."

The pain in my chest and midsection was overwhelming. It felt like I was being tortured by multiple scorching hot steel rods. The bleeding had made its way through my bulletproof vest and onto my army jacket–both were drenched in blood.

I kept thinking to myself, What the fuck is happening? Why hasn't my vest stopped the rounds? That fucker must be using cop killer bullets!

Quickly reached under my vest to keep pressure on the wounds, I realized I was beginning to bleed out. Maximum I had a few minutes before I would pass out and taking a dirt nap. Then it would be off to the afterlife either in Heaven or in my case, more than likely, Hell.

Where the fuck is Rhino? Is he shot up and laying dead in the alleyway?

The only thing keeping me alive was the pure adrenaline flowing through my veins. Thoughts of my family kept smacking me in the face. I could hear and see flashes of their faces.

All of them were screaming at me:

"Get the fuck up now, remember who you are."

"You promised us that you wouldn't get hurt again."

"You told us you didn't even think a bullet could kill you."

"Don't do this to your mother, brother, and sister. Your kids are too small for you to leave them."

At times, on patrol, I did feel invincible–bulletproof. But I knew better than that. I could and had gotten injured badly while performing my duties as a cop. My hand was soaked in blood and my fingers started to stick together from the blood. I pushed my fingers into the bullet holes to slow the blood flow down.

Instead of fleeing the scene, the perp who had just shot me slowly walked toward me. His eyes stare into mine as he said, "Time for you to die. You fucking pig."

He fired two more rounds into me. I felt the bullets pierce

through my ribcage and exit through my back. Shit, my vest didn't even slow the lead projectiles down. I emptied the clip to my 9mm. The bullets came out of my weapon, slowly dropping to the ground. My gun felt like it weighed a hundred pounds. It was like I was in the old Droop-along cartoon.

Then it hit me. I was going into shock. Everything began moving in slow motion. I couldn't hear much of anything–the shots had deafened my ears.

The perp reloaded his weapon, and he mouthed, "You cost me a lot of money arresting my crew. Say goodnight, motherfucker."

Then I saw the muzzle flash from his firearm illuminating the alleyway. The bullet left the chamber at a quarter of its normal speed, and it was heading right for my face. I was frozen, completely frozen in time, unable to move.

I sprang up from bed, drenched in sweat, feeling around for the holes in my body and putting pressure on my various dream wounds. That's when I realized I was still in my jail cell. It had been another nightmare. Unable to move, I stayed seated on the steel bed frame for what seemed like an eternity.

Snapping out of the daze I was in, I slowly laid back down on my prison cot. My eyes just kept staring at the ceiling in the dark. It had been the same nightmare, every single time without fail, since I had been incarcerated. It's the same one I still have to this day.

A tear rolled down the side of my face. I was alone in hell and had no way to get out. My prison sentence had only just started a few months prior.

I just kept praying, "Please God, give me the strength to endure this hellish nightmare. Walk with me and carry me on your shoulders. I don't know if I can make it through this Lord."

Each night while I was incarcerated, I would say the prayer to the guardian of all law enforcement officers. The Archangel Saint Michael. "Defend us in battle. Be our protection against the wickedness and snares of the devil; May God rebuke him.

We humbly pray; And do thou, o Prince of the Heavenly Host, by the power of God, thrust into hell Satan and all evil spirits who wander through the world for the ruin of soul." I needed all the help I could to get.

All I wanted was to get home alive to my family.

CHAPTER TWO

1997 - Before I became an inmate, I was a NYCHA police officer. I patrolled the meanest streets of Uptown Manhattan. During my time on patrol, and in plainclothes, I had arrested and encountered some of the most vicious drug gangs in that section. These are a recollection of the events that took place after I lost my freedom, and what I experienced while serving my sentence.

My time behind bars had changed me as a person. As far as I was concerned, it was all hands-on deck. Prepare for the worst to happen and pray that a miracle got me out alive and returned to my family in one piece.

While I was inside prison, there was no room for me to be a good man. I had to be a no-nonsense hard-boiled ex-cop-convict. It is hard enough to be inside as a regular citizen, but to be incarcerated as a cop, label you as an entirely other entity.

Nothing and no one could have prepared me or the other inmates on how to readjust to the outside world after I was released. It has been over twenty-plus years since I was on my two-year vacation in jail. Yet, every day, I still feel as if I am still shackled to the system. I wrote this book to provide the reader a glimpse into the world that is prison life through a cop's eyes. In no way, shape, or form do I look for self-pity. As the old saying goes, whatever does not kill you only makes you stronger.

The late eighties were a time of complete chaos in the city of New York. Crack cocaine had flooded the streets.

It took hold of its victims, making them commit crimes they normally would have never thought of perpetrating. Crack had raged a war on the people of New York and only a few cops dared to fight against the ruthless drug organizations. Too many, it was a losing battle. But to the few of us, it had to be stopped, by any means necessary. If that meant breaking the rules to win against the enemy and get justice, then so be it. To fight a monster, sometimes you must become a monster. You must think like them and be as ruthless as they are. That's how I saw it, at least. I had stepped into a world I didn't belong in at the ripe age of twenty-two.

I quickly adapted to the surroundings of the people I protected and, at times, would eventually have to arrest. Ultimately, I had become one with that world. It was a violent time in my life, to say the least. The persona I had adopted had taken its toll on me. I had to think like a rogue in order to catch the most dangerous criminals and drug gangs.

That world would later drag me into the pit of hell. I would later call it the big house, the place where I became a prisoner. I learned to live three separate lives, my cop life, my prison life, and my family life. There were many times, and there still are times, that I often struggle with keeping them separated.

CHAPTER THREE

What is the biggest fear a police officer has? It's not the fear of being stabbed, nor is it the fear of getting shot. It's going to prison and facing the inmates he or she once worked hard to put behind bars. That is what cops fear most.

In 1997, I had to stand face to face with the defendants who wreaked havoc on the city I loved. I was another number to the system of New York State. I went from pinning on my shield 3120 to my police uniform to exchanging it for a prison shirt that bore my inmate number 97A-4807. The thoughts that constantly rattled inside my head were a mixture of pure fear, unrelenting anger, and a need to maintain survival mode.

Rikers Island was what I call the training days of my prison life. It is where I would transform myself from being a cop to a convict. What other choice did I have?

It was either become one of them and adapt to prison life or be injured badly or even killed. More than likely, I wouldn't make it out alive. Killing a cop in prison, especially one who had made a lot of criminal's lives a living hell on the street, would be like obtaining a prized trophy.

After a few months on Rikers, the C. O (court officer) called me to the gate.

"Thron, you will be in transit tomorrow morning. You're heading to Downstate."

That night I stayed awake waiting for some bastard to make a move on me and slash my face. Luckily, none of the inmates tried to leave me with a Rikers scar.

Five a.m. came, and I was shackled to a Goliath beast of a man. He had to have weighed 300 plus pounds. The ride to Downstate took several hours. That beast took up most of the bus seat. He smelled like he hadn't showered in weeks. My hell was just beginning that day. As the bus traveled upstate, I kept clenching my hands into fists. My anger boiled to a point where my fingernails began drawing blood from my palms.

The intake officer at the Downstate facility yelled out all our names and ordered us to read off our inmate I. D numbers.

"Thron, step up convict, what is your number?"

"97A4807, sir."

"Don't fucking call me sir."

I was told to strip naked and stand in line to be searched.

The C. O shouted, "Open your mouth and run your fingers through your hair. Now, lift your nut sack. Bend over and spread your ass cheeks, squat five times. Okay, you're clean. Step over to the next station and wait to be called."

The next station was the dreaded shower area. One big room with ten shower heads coming out from the ceiling. I stood in line and was doused with white powder that killed potential lice. While the C.O. threw handfuls of the powder that resembled Ajax, I caught a barrage of it in my face.

As the particles hit my eyes and I heard the officer yell, "Close your eyes, convict, this shit burns like a motherfucker."

Fuck, I thought. It was too late. I was covered from head to toe, front and back. My whole body was burning. It felt as if my skin was going to melt off the bones. I was blinded for what seemed like an eternity, the feeling emulating that of hot embers embedding themselves into my skull. I stood in the line waiting for the water to relieve me and cleanse the poison that clung to my body. My testicles and ass felt like they were being violated by some hell demon.

Finally, I stepped into the shower. "Convicts. Do not step out of that shower room until you hear my command to exit the shower area. Is that fucking understood convicts?"

"Yes, officer."

Finally, it hit me, the blast of freezing ice-cold water. It felt refreshing for an instant. I quickly washed off the powder, which had begun to cake up like dried cement. I cleaned myself off within three minutes. Then I wanted out of the frozen tundra. No dice. I had a few more minutes left.

My body became numb, and my testicles had been sucked up into my stomach. All I could think of was the Seinfeld episode when George's towel fell to the ground and the woman saw his penis and laughed at him. "I'm a grower, not a show-er."

For an instant, it sent a smile to my face and eased the tension in my shivering body. The only thing that entered my mind was: Get me the fuck out of this hell hole, I don't belong in here.

My lips had turned blue, and I was shivering like I was having an epileptic fit.

The guard finally yelled, "Step out of the shower now convicts."

As I exited from the shower room, I looked at the inmates waiting to be sent into the frozen rain shower. I felt their pain.

At the next station an officer handed me two pairs of white boxer shorts, two white tee shirts, two pairs of socks, green pants, a long button-down shirt, one pair of black boots, one pair of white Pro Ked sneakers, and a green jacket. I told myself, when I get out of here, I am never wearing green again.

I dressed as fast as I could to get warm. To be honest, nothing could take the frozen sting out of my bones. It lasted for hours. After I dressed, another officer put me into a holding cell by myself due to being place in P. C (protective custody). P.C. is for any inmates that either have snitched on someone or are high-profile cases. Being a cop put me in that category.

The cell was a six-foot-by-six-foot room made of cinder blocks. There was no bed or bench, nothing except the concrete walls.

If I had to go to the bathroom, I would knock on the cell door and yell, "On the gate." Then, I would be escorted to the John.

I finally fell asleep on the floor after several hours of pacing in the small confines of the cell. I held back the tears that threatened to release from my eyes. I needed to calm myself down and reach deep inside my soul to hide the fear of being killed, or worse, attacked by a gang and sexually assaulted. Being beaten, I could take, but not the latter.

Before I was incarcerated, I made a vow to myself that there would be no way I would allow myself to be touched or made to do any sexual act with an inmate. I was ready to die before letting that happened. And I was going to take a few of them with me.

In my mind, I always tried to keep the wolf's heart and soul. If they thought I was going to be some lame sheep, they had another thing coming their way.

Luckily for me, I was in good enough shape and knew how to handle myself in most hand-to-hand combat situations. I must thank the police department for that and my Aikido training. During my time inside, nothing of that nature ever happened, so I thank God for that every day.

I'd been sleeping on the floor for close to seven hours when I heard the cell door open.

"Get on your feet, convict. You're going to building A."

I was placed inside a filthy corner cell, but the toilet and sink worked, which was a plus as far as I was concerned.

The next morning arrived quickly. My cell door opened, and I was called to a cubical in the middle of the first floor. It had several windows surrounding the four walls with little holes in it to hear the officers speak or vice versa. There were two C.O.'s sitting in the room. One was a Spanish officer; the other was a Caucasian officer. Gallen and Torres were both extremely nice guys.

Gallen spoke to me first. "We read your jacket and know the deal. Do you want to be the floor porter? You will have access to go in and out of your cell all day while you're working."

Torres asked me, "So, do you want the job?"

"Yes, that sounds good to me."

On my tier, I had a cop from the Bronx named Robo who had sexual relations with an underage girl. His cell was on the left side of mine. Then, there was a cop from New Rochelle named Mac on the right side of me. He had been in the wrong place at the wrong time. He was in for a robbery that his friends pulled off.

Unfortunately for Mac, he was driving the car they tried to get away in. Mac and I would become best friends and, more recently, reconnected. The other inmates in the building named that part of our tier EXPO (ex-police officers).

CHAPTER FOUR

Officer Gallen motioned me towards the glass booth. "Pete, you feel like playing some chess?"

"I really have no idea how to play the game."

"Pull up a chair and I will teach you how the game is played. Torres sucks at the game, so I need a worthy opponent."

Gallen taught me the ins and outs of the game, and within a week after learning the strategy of the game, I was able to hold my own against him. It killed the time while I was in Downstate.

Several months later, I saw a young inmate being processed into the building. He couldn't have been more than eighteen years of age. He had a skinny frame and stood about 5'5" in height. Probably weighed 90 pounds while soaking wet.

That afternoon he was sitting by himself eating lunch, so I sat at the table he was eating at and struck up a conversation with him. "Hey how you are making out in here so far?"

He just gave me a nod, basically telling me to fuck off. I downed the bullshit chicken patty and started to get up from the bench, when he introduced himself.

"My name is Mikey. Nice to meet you."

He had two thin scars on his face. One on the right cheek, the other on the left cheek. They ran from the corners of his lips to the midway point of both his cheekbones.

He spotted me looking at them before smiling and said, "That is what you get for snitching."

"Fuck man, I am sorry."

"Don't be. I wanted to play gangster out on the street. I was trying to emulate my father and his mob friends. He's part of a crew on Staten Island."

"Hey Mikey, the first thing you learn here is never let any of these fuck heads know your business on the outside. Especially when it comes to your family."

"I know man I have been in for over a year."

"How old are you, Mike?"

"I'm nineteen turning twenty next week."

"So why did you get green-lit bud?" (That is when an inmate has a hit put out on him or someone wants to prove a point).

"I was talking shit about what my crew did on the streets. Trying to get some street cred in here so I would not have a problem in this shit hole. Somehow, my old friends on the outside heard about me yapping. The next day, they sent me a message to shut the fuck up. I was hit by one of the black gangs. Three of them held me down while the leader of the crew cut me, giving me a joker smiley face. After the scumbag cut me, he whispered in my ear, 'Next time I am going to rape your little ass and you won't be able to walk for a month. Keep your cracker mouth shut or die.'"

A month later, Mikey had told me he was going to be transferred to Clinton Facility. "Pete, I can't wait for this Sunday when my mother comes to visit. Do you need anything from the outside, bro?"

"No man, my family takes care of me with my commissary. My mother and sister try to make it up a few times every month. I'm all good bro, thanks for looking out."

Sunday came and Mikey went to his visit. I was out on the tier mopping the floor when he came back later in the afternoon. There was something off with Mikey. He was walking very gingerly.

He gave me a wink as he walked by me. "Hey Pete, how are you making out today?"

"All is good Mike, how was your visit with your mom?"

"It was great to see her man, really great. She brought me some coffee cakes, cookies, smokes, and new tee-shirts."

"Nice, very happy for you bud."

That night, the C.O. called Mikey to the glass. "Hey, kid, you're being shipped out tomorrow to Clinton. Go to your cell and pack your shit, so you're ready to go in the morning."

About a half hour later, I heard Mikey calling for the porter. That was yours truly. As I approached his cell door, he had his face pressed in between the small rectangle opening of the door. "Yo, bro, I need more toilet paper and paper towels."

"For what Mikey? I just gave you your count this morning."

"Listen, my mother smuggled in a carpenter's knife." He then proceeded to show me the wooden handle curved knife. A multitude of thoughts rushed through my head. Holy mother of God, where the hell did she shove that medieval looking knife? What orifice did she put that thing up?

I looked at Mikey, holding my anger in. What type of son would ask his mother to do something so hideous?

"Mikey, I can't help you, bro. If I get caught with a bad count, I'll be screwed."

"Please, man, I need more paper to cover around it and protect me from being sliced open. Then I can shove it up my ass, so I won't get opened up."

"Are you out of your fucking mind? You crazy prick. If you get caught with that, we will both be thrown into the bing." (The bing is a term used by the inmates for solitary confinement.) I continued, "Sorry man, that's not happening. You are flying solo on this, my man. They catch you with that you're done for."

"Well, if I don't have it to protect myself, I am as good as dead up in Clinton."

"Sorry, brother, I can't help you. Watch your six when you get up there."

"What the fuck is your six, Pete?"

"That's your back, Mikey."

Morning came and Mikey was off to Clinton. He had

an odd walk that day. It kind of looked like he was walking in stilettos. I said a quick Our Father Prayer for my young friend.

Officer Gallen called me in the morning. "Pete, how are the walls in your cell? Are they clean or marked up?"

"To tell you the truth, they are disgusting."

"Do you want to paint your cell today?"

"Absolutely, thank you so much. When can I do it?"

"Torres is having some paint delivered today. When it comes in, help him unload it off the pallet. Then stock it in the closet and you're good to go."

That was a good day. It felt as if I was on the outside doing work on my house. The smell of the paint was euphoric to my soul. For those few hours, I felt like there was a light at the end of the tunnel.

Unfortunately, that light dimmed out rather quickly when I realized I was still incarcerated. Dreams of freedom often only lasted a few moments before reality would set back in.

A few weeks later, I saw another newbie come in. He was a young black man. He held his head down and made sure not to make eye contact with any of the inmates. Some of the hardcore inmates gave their usual howls at him.

"Um, some new meat boys," one yelled out.

"Boy, you better be ready for some loving," another hollered.

Then a low life jerk off yelled, "Bitch, you're going to give me those sneakers and whatever else I want from you."

Torres screamed at them, "Another word out of you convicts, and I will put you all on lockdown for a week."

Then everyone on the tier started screaming, "Shut the fuck up you assholes."

A minute later, all was quiet. It felt like I was in church.

Nobody touched the kid while he was at Downstate. I think they may have actually felt sorry for him. One night during dinner, there was an open seat at the table I was eating at.

The kid was still looking down at the floor and asked me,

"Excuse me, is this seat taken?"

"No, bud, it's all yours. Have a seat and enjoy this crap they call food."

That's when I caught a glimpse of the young man's face. I had never seen such brutal scars on a human being. I tried to keep my composure the best I could.

"Are you the housing cop from Harlem?"

"Yes, how the hell did you know that. How do you know where I worked?"

"I'm from the Lincoln Projects. I heard the stories of the cop named Batman."

"Hey kid, keep that shit to yourself and don't call me that in here, ever."

"Sorry sir, I'm Deshawn. Nice to meet you."

"I'm Pete. Most of the guys call me Porter."

"Is that because you're the tier porter?"

"Yes, that's right, bud. If you need anything in here, let me know. If I can get it for you, I will."

"Anything? Do you mean from the outside world?"

"Listen bud, this isn't Shawshank Redemption in here. I can get you toilet paper and paper towels or hygiene stuff."

"I saw you looking at my face."

"Sorry, bud. The scars just look so angry and inflamed."

"Yeah, I know. They bubbled up because when they were healing, I put Vaseline on them. It made it even worse. I guess you're curious about how I got a tick-tac-toe board carved onto the side of my face."

"I'm not going to lie, kid, I am a little curious."

"I was in the Bloods and I pulled a robbery with a few other crew members. I got caught because my pants got tangled up in a barbed wire fence on Park Avenue. The plainclothes cops from the 25th Pct. caught me. I was looking at 6 to 12 years in prison. The lady we robbed got hurt bad. So, I had no choice but to snitch on them. I had to man. I could not do that much time. Plus, my mother told me if I didn't help the cops and myself, she would disown me."

"So, the Bloods got word to the members in here that I snitched. That's when I got green-lit. They didn't want to kill me. They wanted me to suffer and be left faceless. Well, at least almost faceless. There were six of them when I got surrounded in the shower. They beat the fucking shit out of me first. Then, the biggest one took out a shiv (sharp handmade knife) and carved this tic-tac-toe board on my face. He said, 'Blood in, blood out you, rat bastard.'"

"Shit man. I'm sorry, bud. When you get out, I am sure there is a good plastic surgeon that can help you."

"I hope so, Pete. I am so fucking scared in here, man. I feel like I'm going to get killed in here every time I walk out of my cell."

"Listen, I will talk to Gallen and Torres for you tomorrow. They may be able to help you."

"No don't, I can't afford to be labeled a snitch again."

"Kid just keep your head down and watch your back in here. Stay strong and start to strengthen your body the best you can. Do a lot of pushups and sit-ups, anything that will make your body stronger. A strong mind and body will help you more than you think in here. Try to stay focused and read a lot of books to broaden your mind."

"Thank you for being my friend, Pete."

"Keep your head up kid, you will be okay."

I went back to my cell that night and felt a knot in my stomach. Had any of the inmates heard the kid call me Batman? They only knew that I was a cop, not the housing cop Batman. If word got out to the general population that I was in, I would without a doubt, have a contract put out on me. Some gang members would get himself placed into P.C. to get to me. I had made many perps from the Lincoln houses lives a living hell on the streets of Manhattan.

Now that the kid had opened his mouth, I needed to be on high alert and ready for anything to happen. I needed to speak with the kid in private and make him understand to forget our conversation. I did not want to threaten the young man, but I had no other option. I slept on it that night and decided to wait it out and see what transpired during the next few days.

After a week, I felt confident the kid would keep his mouth shut. I made sure to befriend him. I remembered the old saying from Sun Tzu, "Keep your friends close and your enemies closer."

The fact of the matter was the kid was a Blood. There was no getting around that. I would need to be extra cautious while he was in the house.

One night after dinner I told him, "Kid, don't make a mistake by trying to make a name for yourself in here. If you try to get in the good graces on my behalf with the Bloods, that would be a bad judgement call on your part. Are we clear?"

"Pete, I just want to get the fuck out of here alive."

"Okay, that is all I wanted to hear."

Fortunately, a week later, he was transferred to an upstate facility. I never knew where he went, and I really did not want to know either.

CHAPTER FIVE

The state prisons are also expected to obey the eighth amendment. I will tell you firsthand, some do not. They will push the envelope as far as they can. In my case, the right to be free from excessive bail certainly did not apply to me.

Being that I was a police officer, I was held to a higher standard. My bail was set at the ridiculous sum of one hundred thousand dollars. It was such a mystery to me what the DA's office thought I was into. I had never been in any kind of real trouble when I was young. I was pretty much a clean-cut kid. Maybe they checked my record when I was 16 years old and saw I had been taken in for skinny dipping in a public pool after hours. Other than that, I was never caught doing anything criminal.

Being incarcerated was an incomprehensible mind fuck each day. Not only was I trying to survive the whole ordeal and stay in one piece, but my mind was always thinking about how I had screwed my family over. What were my mother, siblings, and children going through?

I also know I screwed my children's mother over. She was on the force as well and was constantly under IAD's scrutiny.

There wasn't a damn thing I could do while I was incarcerated. I was helpless in helping my family. That is a burden I will forever carry. One of the many sins I am guilty of and will have to answer for when it is time to meet my maker. There had been so many times when I would be lying on my bunk or in the rec room and my mind would start to wander. Countless were the days I did not feel human. Prison just changes a person. Inevitably, someone inside a small cell will become somewhat of a monster. There was no avoiding that for me.

I tried in vain to keep the good in me grounded and keep it

in a safe place, deep inside my heart and soul, hidden away from the other inmates, but that proved to be difficult at times for me.

There was nothing but pure evil and violence around me. Inmates had access to objects around them that could become deadly to other inmates and me. Every other week, the prisoners are given a disposable razor to shave with, as well as toothbrushes to maintain some oral hygiene. If properly put together, the two combined can become one of the most lethal prison weapons.

Although these guys are in prison, they're clever when they want to. The disposable razor can be separated from the plastic holder, the toothbrush is then melted. When the plastic has become soft enough, it is manipulated into a handle for a shank. The inmate then inserts the razor into the toothbrush handle and the blade is then molded in between the plastic. Once the toothbrush has cooled down, the handle is filed down on the concrete floor or wall until the inmate likes how it feels in his hand.

The handle of toothbrushes is also used as weapons when they are filed down into a triangular shape at the tip of the handle. Another way a blade is made is from the filters of cigarettes. They are pressed and melted together. When the inmate has enough butts to work with, the heat turns it into a hard plastic which is then filed down on the concrete. Believe it or not it almost looks like glass.

I can tell you it is certainly as sharp as glass and will cut a person's face just like a razor blade. I was always protective of my face anytime I sat at the end of a table. I would place my hand to the side of my face where it would be exposed to be slashed. I have witnessed the cigarette prison blade used firsthand. It opened a young man's face swiftly, making his cheek look like a hooker's vagina.

When an inmate causes problems, he is placed in solitary confinement. They are in their cell twenty-three hours a day. The one hour they are let out, they are put into a fenced cage no bigger than six-feet by four-feet. They just pace back and forth for exercise.

Does that sound familiar? Those caged convicts were right outside the yard where I trained and walked. I know many of the convicts that are placed in solitary confinement belonged there. I would watch them as if one were watching a lion or a tiger. The pacing back and forth repeatedly. The only difference is it wasn't zoo animals, it was humans.

I need to be clear here. I became a cop for a reason. I was a part of a system to protect the law and if you broke it, you paid the price by going to jail. I was proud of getting drug dealers off the streets. My thoughts were always, If you act like an animal, then you can be treated like one.

However, solitary confinement is more like torture–mental as well as physical. There is no doubt that when I was working and arresting these offenders and getting them off the streets, I truly did not care what happened when they went to prison. But now, I was able to see and experience up close and personal what it is really like to go to prison for charges less than murder or rape.

These guys were no different than I was and were just trying to stay alive, because if you want to survive, it is a 24 hour a day job just to do that. At times, these guys, including myself, had to stay alert in order to stay alive, so if they had to protect themselves, they did it because they were left with no choice.

Unfortunately, they also would also have to pay for that which meant going to solitary. So, in my opinion, when you rape or murder someone you have acted like less than a human and deserve everything you had or have coming to you and should suffer the consequences. However, it was unfortunate that others who may have committed less or were truly innocent of the crimes they were charged with would sometimes end up in the cage.

When a person is placed in a cell with no windows, just four concrete walls, it begins to wear them down. Sure, they can stay somewhat in shape if they choose to, but it's his mind that will begin to lose its ability to stay strong and focus.

When in a cell for so many days and long hours, the prisoner loses track of time and their surroundings. Some will begin to talk to themselves, at times becoming irrational while in solitary confinement. Being placed in the hole or bing, the inmate has extraordinarily little contact with other humans. It will surely have a negative effect on that person's overall health and his brain. It is possible the inmate will suffer from fear and anxiety symptoms while being placed in a cell for twenty-three hours a day. Solitary confinement is the closest form of psychological torture that we know of today and has serious long-term effects on the inmate's health.

My hope is that someday prison officials, lawyers, the judicial system, and legislators come together to really look at the prison system. They need to try and recognize that not all criminals are the same and that not all charges are equal. Therefore, not all situations are the same and should not be treated as such. I would not have ever been able to recognize this unless I was part of both systems.

A person may not have a choice but to use lethality in order to protect themselves and stay alive. Officials do not recognize the emotional injuries in the same way they recognize the physical effects of solitary confinement. The whole system needs to work together to understand the full consequences of these dangerous practices when the prisoner is not there for a serious crime.

True violent offenders will continue to repeat their actions and need to be separated from the non-violent offenders.

Again, I do believe some inmates need to be placed in solitary confinement, if in fact the situation calls for it. What can and does happen is the system creates a non-violent offender into one and then essentially puts them One Under.

CHAPTER SIX

While I was at Downstate, besides training to make my body into a piece of iron, every day I did a thousand pushups and hundreds of ab exercises. I also would do three hundred dips off the edge of my steel cot. There was nothing else to do, and it kept me in tremendous shape.

The only other activity I did often was playing handball. I'll tell you, those games were vicious and highly competitive. What we played for was pride and, of course, cigarettes. It didn't matter that it was a game. Any time, a brawl could break out.

The best players were a guy named Jerry, who was a Bronx gang banger and had scars on his left and right cheek, and an ex-Army soldier named John.

John was a good person who got screwed over by the Army. He told me he was in prison for weapon charges. Something to do with his old army buddies that were still active. I never really understood why he wasn't court martialed.

I remember him saying he'd gotten out with an honorable discharge, but afterwards he did something that wasn't kosher with the army. So, they had him prosecuted by the state. I'm assuming he kept his mouth shut and didn't rat on any of his fellow officers.

Then there was Mac the cop, Robo, and me. The rest of the inmates that played on the handball court were just scrubs. The handballers gave Robo, Mac and I a nickname, the Triple Threat. The games were intense. Torres and Gallen would do side bets with each other.

We would play for two hours every day if the weather permitted. It never mattered if it was hot or cold. It killed some time and kept my mind off the horrible situation I was in.

At night, I would read in my cell. Robert Ludlum and the Jason Bourne books were favorites of mine. I also read the Patricia Cornwell books featuring Kay Scarpetta and the Anne Rice vampire series. There were times when I felt as if I was caught in a recurring nightmare. I'd just stare at the popcorn plastered ceiling, wondering when I'm going to wake up. I'd think of how helpless my family felt and what I had put them through.

To this day, I feel I dishonored my family name. My family assures me I haven't, but the truth is, I did stain it. I made a vow to myself to restore my family's name and that I'd whatever it took to accomplish that.

There were many nights I would lay on the cot and wonder what my children were doing and what they had eaten for dinner. What cartoons were they watching? I pictured them laughing and playing with my two collies.

To tell you the truth, there was no room for those thoughts in prison. I always had to be alert. When anyone is incarcerated, there is an important rule one must follow and keep buried deep in his soul. At any time, your best friend can become your worst enemy. It is the way of the beast in prison.

Being a cop in prison, I had a target on my back. Everyday could be my last day breathing. It was like being a police officer all over again, just a hundred times more dangerous.

I can remember when my mother and sister would come for visits. A few times my cousins also came to keep me company for a few hours. My sister even brought her two daughters to visit me.

Every other Sunday, I would get ready for my get together with my family. I had to hide that I was miserable inside.

So, when I would look into my mother's eyes, I'd tell her and the rest of my family, "Everything is okay. I am safe don't, worry about me."

What the fuck else could I tell them? Deep down we

both knew I was lying my ass off. My mother and sister left my commissary fully stocked every visit. It was a four hour drive each way for them. The worst part was, I wasn't even in my permanent location yet. I had no idea where they would ship me off to next. If Judge Allen and Chief Keen had anything to do with it, I would be shipped off to the furthest location, out of reach to my family.

When the visitation was over, I would be stripped searched for any illegal contraband. During those few minutes it was very humiliating for me as well as the other inmates.

After my visits, I would head back to my cell and check all the things that my family had brought for me. I was like a kid during Christmas morning. I had enough supplies to eat, cigarettes to smoke, and stuff to trade with the other inmates.

I remember a time I was checking to see if the inmates needed any toilet paper or sanitary supplies. There was a Spanish guy named Javier. He was a real punk, a wannabe gangster. He asked me, "Hey Porter, give me a light so I can smoke my loosey." (That is the slang for a single cigarette).

"Sorry bud no can do. I don't have any matches."

"Give me your fucking lighter, bro."

"Let's get one thing straight, I'm not your fucking bro."

A few seconds later Gallen yelled out, "Wrap it up Pete. It's lights out in ten minutes."

"Yes sir, finishing up now."

Javier made a last-ditch effort. "Come on, Porter. Help me out."

"Seriously man I'm not getting thrown into the bing over a lighter."

I hit my cot and started playing solitaire. A few minutes later I heard Torres's yell out. "Lights out in five, convicts."

I hated when they called us convicts. It pissed me off so damn much. I kept telling myself you are not a convict. But again, I had to always think like one while I was incarcerated. I truly had no other choice. I'd often think, it's not the violence that controls a man. It's the distance he's willing to go.

I had taught myself during my police career and while I was in prison to control my fear. Or else it could get me killed. I would hone it into a weapon and stay alive. That's not to say I wasn't scared in prison, I was. But I had to keep the fear inside and never show it to anyone, or at least die trying.

Right before Torres hit the lights, bam, what appeared to be a gun shot rang out. I went to my cell door.

Mac was already at his. "What the fuck was that Mac?"

"I have no idea, brother."

The lights to the whole tier went out. We were in the dark. In the rear of the unit, I heard a person screaming.

"Help me! I am burning."

Gallen and Torres raced over to the cell door where the screams had come from. It was Javier, he was burnt badly along his face and neck. The officers couldn't get to him. The locks to all our cells were permanently in their secured positions.

I heard Gallen ask Javier, "What the hell happened to you?"

Javier cried out loudly, "I was trying to light my cigarette with a paperclip but when I put it in the outlet it exploded in my face."

Torres yelled at him, "You stupid motherfucker! You killed all the electricity in the entire building. You could have killed yourself."

Luckily, they had a generator brought up to the floor and were able to get Javier out of his cell. He was taken to the medical ward and treated for the burns he acquired.

Torres politely announced, "Your friend Javier just cost all of your rec privileges for a week. You can thank him when you see him. That is if you ever see him. If I get my way, he will be shipped out of here before the sun rises."

I never saw that idiot again. I learned quickly not to screw around with the C. O's.

CHAPTER SEVEN

During that week of our punishment, I was still working as the porter of the block. One afternoon I heard Torres announce, "New meat coming in convicts. Treat him with respect and no funny business. If anyone gives him a problem, I will add another month to the lockdown that has already been put into place. Do you all understand me?"

"Yes, sir."

Two C.O.'s from intake escorted the new inmate onto the tier. I gave a quick look as he passed by.

Holy fuck, I thought to myself, is that Cesar Hilario from the Red Top Crew?

I gave Gallen a wave to let him know I was heading back to my cell.

My heart was pounding, and it felt like I was going to have a heart attack. I sat up on my cot and began to breathe slowly. It took a few minutes before I was able to calm myself down. Needing to keep myself occupied from the thoughts that were swirling around inside my head, I figured working out was the best thing I could do.

After a few hundred bed dips and pushups and sometime staring into the plastic mirror in my cell, sweat beaded down my forehead.

Time to get fucking serious, brother. Do what you must to get home to your kids and family. That is all that matters. If it is Cesar, just be ready to go to fucking war.

I laid down on my cot and closed my eyes reflecting on the case against Hilario.

He was a ruthless bastard. He was one of the top clockers

in the neighborhood. Clockers are drug crews that deal 24-7. Cesar had dealt crack to young children, pregnant women, basically anyone that wanted a hit of the rock demon. He didn't have a care in the world. The drug game was his life, and he would have sold dope to his own mother. He needed to be taken down, and I was going to be the cop that took his ass in.

I was still in uniform working with my partner in the condition's car. My operations lieutenant gave me free rein in all the sectors that our command covered. Cesar was the under-boss of the Red Top Crew that operated on 2nd Avenue and 118th Street.

That was a big problem for me, his operation was off project. Stupid ass rules of the housing brass.

The bosses would constantly say, "Make your collars on the project grounds. Stop making off project arrests."

That shit just didn't sit well with me. Drug dealing on or off project grounds was against the law last time I checked. And I loved making narcotics arrests. So, I tossed that order out the window.

The only housing project near there was the Wagner houses on 120th Street. I would need an excuse as to why I was doing recon on the street, especially in a building that was off project grounds.

It was my fifth day at work. I would be falling into three day (RDO) regular days off. I decided to let the Red Top Crew do their business for the night. I would return to the street on my day off in plainclothes.

The next morning, I grabbed my army jacket and drove into Manhattan from my Brooklyn home. At that time, I was driving a 73 Javelin, which I restored the entire body and chassis. That car was a badass vehicle. It looked like the Mad Max Interceptor cruiser. And it was extremely fast. When my foot hit the gas pedal; it just took off like a bat out of hell.

I parked the car on the corner of 120th and Second Avenue at around 10 a.m. I took a quick inspection of who was out on the corner where the Red Top Crew controlled.

One thing for sure, it was going to be a long day on the rooftop that I had selected to perform my recon on.

I grabbed my supplies and equipment and headed to my perch. The building walls were covered in graffiti. The Red Top and Black Top crews had formed an alliance and took the building over, marking their territory.

The tenants lived in fear of being beaten or robbed or assaulted. Some elected to move out of the entire neighborhood. The drug organizations had taken over several of the apartments, so I needed to tread lightly while I made my way up to the rooftop.

The elevator was a human toilet and stunk of piss and crap. I walked up the flight of stairs slowly, but the boards were creaking loudly. I took deep breaths when I heard a door open, my off duty six shooter by my side, ready for action if the situation arose.

I was invading their territory; even worse, I was off duty. If something went down, I would have all sorts of problems. The main problem would be explaining why the hell I was doing a recon on my day off. I just thought, no risk, no reward. Collaring the Red Top Crew would be my reward.

I reached the roof and settled in for the day. I had heard from one of my informants that Cesar had shot several people with the Raven 25 automatic he always carried on him. A lot of gang members liked to carry that weapon because it was small and easy to shoot. It was also a cheap weapon and held six rounds in the clip. The word out on the street was, he was also rather good with a butterfly knife.

I had an extremely reliable informant on my private payroll at the time. A man I called Cyclops. He was the lieutenant in the Red Top Crew. He was also their enforcer. When I collared Cyclops, he had a ton of vials on him, several months earlier. He agreed to cooperate with me and give me details on other crews operating on the Four Corners on Second Avenue.

117th Street to 119th Street along Second Avenue was a fucking candy land for the addicts. There was heroin and crack on every corner. So, I came up with the nickname the Four Corners.

By 11 a.m., the street started to come alive. I could hear all the lookouts on their assigned corners yelling out, "Black top, greys, pinks and red top. We got three and five-dollar jumbos. Get 'em while it's hot."

I had observed my C.I. coming out from a building on Second Avenue and directed his people to their positions. Second Avenue was extremely busy for the next three hours. The clockers were making a ton of money for their crews. I observed Cyclops re-up his dealer four times.

At one p.m., I caught a break and spotted Cesar riding up on a bike which had a bell on the handlebars. He rang the bell while skidding on the sidewalk as he approached Cyclops who then handed him a wad of money. In return, Cyclops took a brown paper lunch bag from Cesar.

I thought to myself, I should have done the recon in my car that way I could have followed Hilario back to his stash house.

I waited it out until the crews started to change shifts to exit the building. Leaving would be a lot harder. I walked as quietly as possible down the stairs. The stench of urine hit my nostrils. How do the tenants put up with this shit?

I made it back to my Javelin and sat for a while in my car. I knew the answer to my own question, it was total fear. The Four Corner crews had them all scared shitless. Cesar became an obsession for me.

I started to use different surveillance tactics during the course of my investigation. I would use the rooftops or sit in the RMP (radio motor patrol car) waiting for him with my binoculars. For several weeks there was no site of Cesar.

Then on one 4-12 shift, my partner and I were heading down Second Avenue when we spotted Cesar being dropped off by a gypsy cab. He bolted right into a building along the

Avenue. I knew there was no way in hell I would be able to explain to the brass why I kicked a door in without a warrant off-project. Cesar Hilario was a crafty SOB. We would have to wait another day to snatch his ass up.

For the next few days, I watched how the Red Top crew captain was transporting his bundles and dropping the narcotics to his crew.

Cesar was one rank below the boss, Gonzo. I ultimately arrested Gonzo later that year. Gonzo was another case I mentioned in End of Tour.

I kept pressing my C.I. for as much information on his crew as he'd give up. I usually got the same response. "Batman, if they even think I am snitching on them, I am as good as dead. After they are finished killing me, they for sure will kill my brother and mother."

"Okay, bud, just remember, I know you have at least two hundred vials on you right now. That is a B felony charge. That will make you a three-time loser and then it's life in prison. So, keep the information coming on all the other crews. Or by the hand of God, I will drop the hammer down on your ass. Are we clear on that?"

"Yes, Batman. All is good, I got you."

Hilario kept eluding me until one 4-12 shift. I spotted him coming out of a building on 116th Street and Lexington Avenue. He was holding a brown paper lunch bag.

I yelled to Hondo who was driving, "There he is, it's Cesar! Let's go, brother. He's holding."

Cesar was riding his bike and if I had anything to do about it, that would be his final bike ride for a long time.

"Get me as close as possible to that fucker, so I can hit him with the car door as he is riding down the street."

Hilario had ridden fast enough to get a half block distance between us. "Hondo, floor it. Put the pedal to the metal, brother."

We rolled up on him. When he spotted us over his left shoulder, ringing his little bike bell playing innocent. I rolled down my window and said, "Nice bike, bud."

"Thank you, Batman. Have a good day."

He took off and tried to cut between two parked cars. Hondo was right behind him. I had my door opened and slammed into the back wheel of the bike sending him crashing into a parked car. Cesar, and the vials, crashed to the ground.

As I approached him, he put his right hand inside his coat pocket, fumbling for what I knew was either the butterfly knife or the 25-automatic pistol.

"I wouldn't do that, son. I promise you; I'll put one between your eyes." He knew I wasn't bluffing about shooting him.

He just threw his hands up and said, "You got me, Batman."

I cuffed him up and started searching him. I retrieved the 25 automatic pistol and 800 red top vials of crack. That arrest happened a few year priors to my incarceration. Cesar had plead out opting not to go to trial. He was sentenced to five years. That arrest was his second violent felony.

I laid on the cot thinking of a plan, deliberating on if in fact it that scumbag was. If it was, I would have no choice but to make a move on him during dinner time. My heart was pounding, and I was extremely nervous about being shanked or sliced across my face.

Prisoners that were doing a long stint had nothing to lose and would have cut or stabbed me. It would have given them jailhouse cred to leave me with a scar. It would also be a warning to show me who was in charge inside.

Outside on the streets, I had the shield and gun, that gave me the upper hand. It also didn't hurt to be a member of the biggest gang in New York–twenty-eight thousand men and women in blue.

Gallen cracked my door to get the tables ready for dinner. I walked to the glass booth and said, "Officer Gallen, the new inmate might be a guy I collared a few years ago."

"What do you want to do, Pete?"

"Can you give me his name, Gallen?"

"No, I can't do that Pete. Remember this is protective custody."

"Okay, if it is him, I'll have to take care of business, or I will have problems in here."

"Hey, just try to keep cool for the time being. I will alert Torres about this."

At five p.m., Torres cracked the cells open and yelled. "Chow time. Lets go, time to eat." I watched as the newbie exited his cell and began walking down the stairs to the main floor.

This time, I got a good look at him and immediately clenched my right fist. I was ready to drop a hammer on him if I had to. To my relief the guy just looked like Hilario, it wasn't him.

Thank God for small miracles. He was a small-time felon who did a burglary. He wasn't a bad guy to my surprise. If it had turned out to be Cesar Hilario, it would have created more than a few problems for me.

CHAPTER EIGHT

The transition from being a cop to an ex-con was extremely grueling for me. It was a total mind fuck emotionally. I was fine with the physical part of it, but the most challenging part was keeping my mind clear and my heart and soul strong. I can remember the first several months lying on my steel cot just staring at the ceiling. I'd often glance towards my cell door, my eyes fixating on the door handle.

More times than not I pictured myself wrapping a bed sheet around my neck, tying the knot tight enough to cut off as much circulation as possible to my brain, then tying the other end of the bed sheet to the door handle and slowly sliding down the back of the door to hang myself.

For months, I had wanted to end the pain and shamefulness I had brought upon my family. Every night I'd conjure those images and would ultimately end up thinking about my father.

When I was eleven months old, he took his own life. My mother had decided when he died, she would protect my brother, sister, and me from the horrible truth about our father. From what I understand, my entire family vowed to keep his death a secret to protect us. I come from the Sicilian family of Volpe's and Valente's. That is my mother's side.

My father's side was made up of doctors the Thron's and Dondero's. First came my grandfather who was a very dedicated physician. He would still be making house calls in the Bronx at the late age of eighty years old. The street he lived on was later named, Thron Way. Then, my father's brother became a doctor.

Lastly, was my father, who would become a podiatrist.

While in medical school, he had developed gallstones and refused to get them taken out. He was at the end of his final year in medical school and wanted to finish it out before having the stones removed. So, he opted to take pain medicine instead.

He would end up being named the Salutatorian of his class. That achievement came with a high price–he became addicted to the painkillers. He had become a functional working drug addict. He never went into the hospital to have the gallstones taken out.

It was a very asinine move on his part because my grandfather could have easily performed the surgery. Instead, he decided to keep taking the pain medicine and would end up making my life a living hell.

My heart goes out to my mother, brother, and sister because of the perdition he brought down on our family. My brother would later tell me in detail his memories of my father nodding out at the kitchen table. My mother, the saint that she is, would try to protect her husband's image in my brother's eyes and tell him, "Dad is just tired from work."

One time, he had taken my brother with him to the Bronx to visit my grandparents. After the stopover with his parents, my uncle Dickie, who was a built man standing at 6"2' weighing 240 pounds, tried to grab my father's keys from him and said, "Ronny, hang out for a little while and let the alcohol wear off a bit. I don't want you driving with my nephew while you're intoxicated."

He ended up pushing my uncle to the floor saying, "Give me the fucking keys, Dickie."

My father was strung out from not being able to get any drugs, so he opted to drink instead until he acquired more drugs.

As he headed to our Long Island home, he took the Throggs Neck Bridge. My brother, who was about 6 or 7 years of age at that time, told me, "Pete, I remember sitting in the backseat looking out the window and seeing sparks flying off the hubcaps. Dad kept steering the car into the wall."

His selfishness had put his own son's life in imminent danger, and he didn't give a damn. There was one memory my brother had that haunt him to this day. My father was so whacked out on Demerol that he wasn't able shoot it into his arm himself. So, he proceeded to show my brother how to inject the syringe instead.

The memories my brother carries are horrific to say the least. Fortunately, my sister and I had been spared of those horrendous memories. My mother would tell us of the beautiful times they had with each other, about the love that they shared when he was alive.

We were originally told that he had died in a car accident. I know in my heart it was to protect us. My mother is the true protector of our family.

After my father had taken his own life, the Thron's disowned us. They sold all my father's doctor's equipment, got rid of his office, and kept every cent they made from it for themselves.

I cannot even begin to fathom what the weight of keeping this family secret was like for my brother and sister–they had found out the truth many years before me. I often wondered how many times my family looked into my eyes wanting to reveal the secret of my father but held true to their vow of silence.

That is what a strong family does: they protect their young at any price–I get that protective soul from my mother and siblings.

When I was young, the Volpe's were my mother's side of the family. My grandmother and grandfather would become like second parents to us. My grandfather ruled the entire family with an iron fist. It didn't matter whose house we were at for the holidays, his word was final. That was the law of the land as far as he was concerned.

My aunts and uncles would all become major parts in my life. I would watch the Volpe ladies of the house cook dinners and bake. Through my grandfather and uncles, I would learn the values of family and life. My cousins turned into siblings.

I honestly don't know of a stronger family than the Volpe's. I consider myself an incredibly lucky man.

On those tempting nights inside my prison cell, I would hear all their voices telling me, "Stay alive and keep fighting."

The problem in the beginning was the fight inside my soul. The dark half wanted out of that miserable hole, even if it meant going straight to hell for committing suicide. There would be one good thing if I went to hell, I would get to face my father.

In my heart and soul, I hate the man. Not for what he did to me, but for what he did to my mother and siblings. I can never forgive him for his sins against my family. However, it could very well have been a blessing in disguise because realistically if he'd lived he would have continued using.

Later, in life I would plead with God to forgive him for his sins and bring him to heaven. For me, I will never forget or forgive, but I wanted my mother to finally have peace in her mind. When I do finally meet my father, in heaven or hell, he will answer for all his sins against my loved ones.

The good side of my soul would always end up prevailing because I never wanted to put my mother and siblings or the Volpe family another premature death like that again. My father's death was hard on everyone in my family. Plus, there was always my heart, my three children who I had to make it home to.

As the months passed while I was Downstate, I had finally conquered the emotional roller coaster. There was no way I would be going out that way. If I were to die in prison, it would be through battle or sickness, not suicide. I had to stay strong mentally and physically.

I can tell you one thing, when you are caged like an animal, your mind plays tricks on you. It is always testing your spirit to live. It takes hold of your soul and tries to drain you of any life left inside of you. I decided I had to bring back my beliefs in the art of meditation through Zen.

Every day, I would kneel on the floor as long as possible,

emptying my mind. Then, I pictured the world I wanted to be in when I was released. I taught myself to ignore the pain that the hard floor brought upon my knees. Nothing mattered to me, except getting home to protect my children from the evilness of the world. They deserved to have their father home with them. The only thing that would stop me was myself. I would never do to them what my father did to me and my family.

Inside the cell, I found myself talking to the air as if my soul was outside my own body. Giving it commands and instructions on how to survive in prison, even rationalizing with it.

While being incarcerated, I learned to sleep with one eye open. There was no room for heavy sleep, only lightly dozing off. I was always on the ready for anyone or anything to jump off and try to kill me or attack me. I left no room for error. Only the strong survive and the weak quickly become prey. I refused to ever let myself be at the mercy of another. I would die fighting if I had to.

Being incarcerated also showed me the power of words. I must thank my ATF training for that. While I was an investigator for that unit, I learned how to properly interrogate some of the most dangerous drug organizations in New York City.

When I was inside, I used that knowledge to help keep me alive. It meant befriending men who in my other life I would be at war with and arresting. My communication skills would prove to be the most powerful weapon in my arsenal while in prison.

CHAPTER NINE

When I stood before Judge Allen to be sentenced, I never looked down at my feet. The little voice inside my head kept saying, don't let this man win, stare directly into his eyes. You know you're innocent. Don't let this son of a bitch strip you of your pride and dignity.

The judge had fire in his eyes. He was in complete control of my life, and he was going to make me pay for insulting his intelligence. That was due to the letters my friends and family had written for me.

Allen deepened his voice and announced my sentence with the evilest of intentions. "The defendant was found guilty by a trial of his peers. Sir, you are sentenced to one and a half to four years in prison. You will be remanded to a Medium prison facility."

I hear those words every day in my head and the rage that followed will never leave me. I bury them deep inside my soul, like those feelings for my father. I learned in life to let many things go, but those two things I will never have any mercy for. Both incidents did irreparable damage to my immediate family, for that there will be no negation or forgiveness.

When people watch TV shows that have prison content, the show often portrays what prison is like so that people will find it entertaining. But those are just actors, and their experience isn't actually real.

When ordinary people see the fences that surround the walls of a prison, they are probably wondering, what and who are behind those heavy guarded walls? What did the men behind them do to get placed inside there? Behind the walls of any penitentiary, it is another world. I would not wish that hellish nightmare on my worst enemy.

The truth of the matter is, I was the cop who put the bad guys away in silver bracelets. There was no better feeling in my life then when I would observe a drug transaction go down. The feeling of being on a rooftop looking down on the violent drug gangs as they performed their business knowing I would be taking them into custody within a few minutes by any means necessary was so euphoric to me.

I believe that feeling is like the one IAB and Judge Allen felt when I was the one put in silver bracelets. They fed on bringing cops down. The IAB cops were in that unit for only two reasons.

The first is that they themselves had gotten caught doing something wrong. So, they sold out the cops they knew were corrupt and hung them out to dry.

The second reason is that IAB is the quickest way to getting a promotion, especially for a member of the service who is on a list to become a higher rank. He or she will learn how to burn cops. Handing out rips, also known as complaints, against a police officer. It becomes second nature to them when they arrive at their new assignment.

As for Judge Allen and Judge Andrews, who had handled my earlier hearing cases then my appeal, bending the rules of the court and the law was second nature to them.

As the correction officer placed the cuffs onto my wrists for the very first time during my incarceration, I felt a piece of my soul slowly die. Walking down the corridor with my hands behind me was so surreal to me. I kept closing my eyes and opening them to awaken me from the nightmare I must have been having.

I heard my voice screaming, "Well, I will be a monkey's uncle, you're in the worst jam you've ever been in. How are we getting out of this one? Maybe we can break these steel cuffs and run and get the fuck out of here."

When I was put in my first cell, my world changed from the moment the door closed behind me. There were so many times inside I wanted to give up and end it. I am one of the lucky ones, my vigor was strong, my mind was able to have the fighting spirit of a samurai. That I was fortunate enough to have learned from my family, and my sensei in Aikido training. When I trained in prison, I had only one choice, it was to forge my body into a piece of Iron. I had to if I were to engage in combat. There was always a good chance of that happening, and I needed to be prepared for the worst.

While training, I would picture the Spartan soldiers pouring the melted down steel into a cast made of cement to make a blade, forging their blades into a piece of weaponry like no other. The Spartans' blades were the strongest of all fighters. That image burned itself into my mind.

I saw my body as a blade made of fire and ice, making a vow to myself never to let anyone inside to break my mind or body. I knew in my heart and soul there would be no way of avoiding confrontations. The words that I spoke to other inmates needed to hit home. Otherwise, I would be in a different altercation each day.

I can remember the feeling of seeing the razor fencing that was wrapped around the walls of the prison for the first time. It scared the living shit out of me. I had seen these types of barbed wire fences before while chasing criminals in the streets of Harlem.

But that feeling was different when I was pursuing a criminal–it felt like pure adrenaline. Back then, when I needed to climb over a barbed wire fence, it meant nothing to me. The possibility of getting entangled in the fence was a necessary evil. There was one on-foot pursuit in which that exact situation happened. Sure, I suffered some lacerations, but the fear of being sliced open never even entered my mind. All I felt was the rush of making an arrest.

The chill that came over me the instant that fences came into view was bone shattering. At that moment, I knew my freedom had been torn from me. My body had lost all its energy.

The feeling of the cold concrete as I sat in my first cell dulled my senses and my will to survive. I will always remember the first time my hands wrapped around the cold steel bars of the cell I was thrown into.

I immediately remembered telling so many of the people I had arrested, "You better get used to that view from inside."

Now the correction officers would be repeating those words to me. Karma is a bitch, that is for sure. Still, I knew the perpetrators I collared deserved to be sent to jail for breaking the law. They were committing crimes and had to be taken in and answer for the crimes they had perpetrated.

Thinking back as I write this book, maybe I was punished for being a bit of a rogue cop.

There were many times I felt the rules and regulations of the police department were just ridiculous, so I bent them in order to enforce the law. I would tell myself, "The guys that make up these stupid rules are pencil pushing jerkoffs. They're nothing but desk jockeys they know nothing about the streets."

I would hear officer Sena's voice saying to me, "Kid, all that book shit you learned in the academy, throw it out the fucking window."

Just maybe that's why I was punished. I may have been too heavy handed or too gung ho. On the streets, I needed to be that way to get home safely. It was them or me. It is the way of the mean streets of NYC.

As I began to settle into life as a convict, there were many things I would hear and observe. During the nighttime, I would hear inmates weep about wanting to go home, asking God to help them.

The hardened inmates would shout, "Shut the fuck up you pussy."

When I would tear up or weep, I did it in complete silence. Luckily, those feelings only lasted the first few months.

I had become one with my surroundings assimilating myself into their world. I have been fortunate enough in my life to gain the ability to adapt to anything. Any new place or new city I lived in was easy for me to get accumulated to.

Jailhouse food was not the greatest, so I learned to improvise and season all that crap they served. The best days in prison were when my floor would go down to get commissary every other week. My mother and sister always put money in my commissary so I could shop.

I had a good cellmate who was also an ex-cop, and we had no problem sharing the food between the two of us. There wasn't a month that we didn't have at least four cartons of cigarettes in our cabinets. We were both lucky to have our families come up twice a month and bring in food and smokes from the outside world.

Mac and I were both devout Catholics and would do prayers at three p.m. every day. I would do the rosary which usually would take me twenty minutes. It was our ritual. It kept us connected to God.

Most days while I was inside, I would wonder what my kids were doing during the day. Were they watching cartoons or playing with their toys? Those years could never be replaced. I kept replaying the night in question.

One question stood out: What could I have done differently?

The answer was simple. I would have completed the drug transaction and arrested the dealer and the buyers. No one would have been given a break that night. All the perps would have been taken into custody. My decision to let the two men that were loitering to buy drugs go would never have happened. They were lucky and got a get out of jail free card that night. That was a huge mistake on my part, I would pay for it and still am today.

The sad truth is, there are no take backs in the narcotics game. You act or react to complete the mission that day or night. However, the cards fall, that is the hand you're dealt.

On the outside, people sleep to rest and recuperate from

their daily activities to cope with the stresses of life. While incarcerated, falling sleep was an enemy to me. If I were in a dorm with other inmates and fell asleep, there was a good chance something would happen. I learned to sleep with one eye open.

On the other side of the spectrum, if I fell asleep in a cell where I didn't have to worry about being hit or killed, I would have constant nightmares. If I had a good dream or just a good night sleep, which was rare, I would wake up in the cell realizing I wasn't a free man. I still had to do my time.

The days and nights dragged out. A day felt like a week, and a week felt like a month. My memories of prison have become my monsters and demons that I live with every day. I can assure you these monsters and demons are real to me.

My daily routine when I arrived at my permanent facility, Cayuga, was repetitive but very necessary. It kept alive.

I worked down at Z block during the morning and dinner time. Afternoons, I would work in the mail room. Every morning I woke up at 4:30 a.m. to perform seven hundred pushups. After I was finished, I would wake up Mac for our morning cup of coffee. Then at 6:00 a.m., I headed downstairs to be frisked and searched for possible weapons. It was ridiculous, they knew I wasn't carrying any contraband. I guess it was protocol for them.

After I finished doing my work in the morning, I'd always have enough time to do another three hundred pushups. One of the officers who I was friends with was nice enough to install a pull-up bar for me.

At my peak, I was doing three hundred pull-ups, a thousand ab movements, and a thousand pushups. Then, there was two hours in the yard to lift weights. The prison yard would turn out to be the most dangerous times of my stay at Cayuga.

CHAPTER TEN

In any prison, the yard is by far the most dangerous of places in a penitentiary. At any time, a violent incident could occur. The gang members had their own circles. The Latino inmates consisted of several gangs, the MS-13, Neta's, Mexican Vatos Loco's, Latin Kings, Dominican's Don't Play (DDP). They controlled one side of the yard while the black gangs, the Crips and Bloods controlled the other side. The white inmates were basically in the middle.

I stayed as neutral as possible, trying to avoid any type of conflict. The problem was, if a gang member wanted to earn their stripes and move up in the ranks, I could be the target of a hit.

I mainly trained with weights in the yard by myself, on occasion I would train with a big Bronx banger named, Tito.

One cold winter night, I was training with my buddy, Tito, when all hell broke loose. In the far corner of the yard, we could hear two rival gang members arguing. The first inmate was a Latin King who bore several jail-house tattoos. The crown tattoo on his arm had five points and is the symbol of the Latin Kings gang. He also donned three tear drops under his right eye. Which meant only one thing, he had killed three people, either on the streets or in prison. He went by the name Wilder. The man barely spoke a word, he just mumbled. Every smart inmate knew to avoid him, or they might become a new tear drop on his face.

The second inmate was a short and pudgy man named Aiden. He had curly black hair and was a member of the Vatos Locos, a Mexican gang. These two gangs were enemies in the streets.

Apparently, Aiden heard Wilder mumble something in his direction and confronted him. He was holding a twenty-pound dumbbell at his side. After several minutes of testing each other's machismo, Aiden tried to crack the Latin Kings head, but he missed his mark hitting Wilder's shoulder with the dumbbell. The Latin King grabbed a long barbell and swung at Aiden's head connecting, affectively cracking and fracturing his skull open.

Seconds later, all the inmates and I were ordered to hit the pavement face down. Over the loudspeaker from the guard tower, a marksman shouted into a megaphone, "Stay on the ground with your head down against the pavement. If anyone moves, you will be shot."

After the mayhem was over, we were placed in lock down for a week as punishment. Wilder beat the charges of assault in the first degree because it was deemed self-defense. He was out of the hole within a month and back to mumbling under his breath. Aiden never stepped foot back on the tier. They had transferred him to another location. He probably was a vegetable by the time he reached his new destination.

Back at Downstate, I remember playing handball with a few of the inmates. On the court there was plenty of shoving and various elbows being thrown. At times, an elbow or two would find a part of an inmate's face.

I was involved in many arguments and shoving matches. Nothing really every came of those incidents. Looking back now, it was merely a way of testing one's courage not to back down from an altercation. All the players wanted to claim the handball court as his domain.

One summer day, we had stopped for a water break, when we saw the inmates from the general population heading to the softball field. I could not believe my eyes when I saw several of the inmates were carrying baseball bats.

I kept asking my buddy John, "What the fuck are the C.O.'s

thinking letting them have bats?"

Within ten minutes of the game, a few Spanish inmates were swinging the bats at other rival gang members. It was a total rumble on the softball field. Bodies were being tossed in the air while others were being pummeled into the ground. The orange crush, the SWAT team for the prisons, was called into restore order. I would have to say approximately eleven inmates were seriously injured, and some even suffered lacerations and broken bones.

The games I played in during yard time were both physical and brutal. I wasn't much of a basketball player. I never really liked the sport, but I would occasionally play some hoops to kill time.

The entire game was made up of fouls, elbows, and pushing matches. Every inmate that played suffered bruises and cuts, some even suffered a broken nose or finger. The yard was just-plain insanity. Every time I stepped out onto the exercise yard, I knew my chances of being shanked or killed increased.

I mainly used the yard for the weights and to walk along the quadrangles outside the perimeter. There was a group of us that walked or jogged the parameters. It was a means for us to take in the birds and trees. The sites of the world outside the barbed wire fences let me hold onto hope. I saw freedom beyond those fences, all I had to do was survive and do my bid without getting involved in any incidents. That would prove to be an extremely hard mission to accomplish.

I'd given myself the hardest undercover assignment that I would ever be involved in. I had to become one of them and somehow remain true to myself and keep the good in me. I knew who I was in reality; a father of three small children, a son, and a brother to my sibling's, also an uncle. A sixty second decision that I had made turned all their lives upside down. I made a vow to atone for that sin. To this day, I've not accomplished that yet. But I still have a lot of time. I didn't know it then, but I also was fighting to get out and meet the woman of my dreams. Adriana, who is my miracle come true.

I remember an incident while playing in a handball death match game. That was our nickname for it because it was so physical. My partner for the game was an ex-Army soldier named John. He was one of the nicest guys I ever had the pleasure of knowing. He was so soft spoken and had a wealth of knowledge at his disposal. I was much older but we both had seen combat. He had been in battles during his military time. I had been involved in the war on drugs in our homeland New York. We would trade war stories hanging onto the lives we once had and loved. I called him Johnny and he would call me pop.

We were matched up against two drug gang members. Jerry and Acosta, they were serving ten-year bids. Those two convicts were involved in some serious shit on the street. Both also made it known that they were bad asses in the Boogie Down Bronx.

I remember an old saying while I was inside and working as a cop, "Always be careful of the quiet guy. He is the most dangerous person of all. He never lets anyone know the hand he is holding".

I tried in vain to be the quiet guy. I would always hear my brother's voice saying, "Pete, don't fuck with the quiet ones. They're the most dangerous people."

Sound advice and I live by his words to this day. I passed my brother's insight onto my two boys as well.

The game began, and we were at each other's throats from the very start. The score went back and forth until it was tied up and whoever scored the next point would win. The prize was four packs of smokes each. Jerry slammed a low serve and Johnny returned it with a crushing blow. The handball sailed high into the air and had stuck into one of the razors which was wrapped around the fencing. The rubber ball was about seven or eight feet from the ground dangling on the razor tip. That's when Johnny made a huge mistake. He jogged over to the fencing and jumped up to smack the ball to free it from the razor fencing. The ball fell and rolled on the cement, but Johnny's hand suffered a deep laceration. That was just the beginning of his and our problems.

The guard tower that overlooked both yards general population and pc had observed Johnny jumping up. Ten seconds later I heard the familiar sounds of shotguns being racked and loaded. The bull horn sounded off, "Get the fuck down on the ground or you will be shot on site and charged with escape."

I laid spread eagle with my hands above my head and face down on the concrete handball court. The orange crush rushed into the quad, pinning all our heads with their boots against the cement, ordering us to stay still.

They picked Johnny up and slammed him into the fence and cuffed his legs and arms with a daisy chain that wrapped around his waist. He was hog tied to prevent him from running. They actually thought that soldier was trying to escape. Johnny was bleeding very heavily. The crush escorted him to the infirmary ward to get stitched up. That night, we were locked in without any rec privileges.

Days went by, still no sight of my buddy, Johnny. I asked officer Gallen, "What happened to John?"

"He was charged with attempted escape which is a felony."

"Come on your kidding me, the guy just tried to get the ball off the razor tip. He had six months left on his term and was going home."

"He isn't going anywhere now, they added three more years to his sentence, and he was transferred to a max."

"Sorry, Officer Gallen, but that is just plain fucking wrong. He wasn't trying to escape. You know, that right?"

"Pete, let me give you some sound advice. If you want to go home quickly just worry about yourself. You aren't one of these guys, remember that and stay focused on the light at the end of the tunnel."

"Copy that, sir, it's your move."

CHAPTER ELEVEN

Cops and criminals have different eyes than the average person. For the most part, I can always tell if a person is a cop. Their stare is very distinctive. It is as if the men and women in law enforcement can look right through a person's eyes and tell if they're up to no good.

As a cop, and even today, I'm able to see everything around me regardless of where I am. I've ingrained that mindset to my children and my future wife that they should always be looking around them wherever they are.

Cops often have this keen intellect for knowing when danger lurks near them–at least that's the way it was for me. That comes with training and field experience. I am extremely fortunate to be good friends with the most decorated detective in the NYPD history, Ralph Friedman. Ralph is the cop I would want with me in a time of battle. His detection of right and wrong and pure courage is second to none. The man is a true hero, and I am honored to know him and have learned from him in the short time we've been friends.

Growing up my brother was a fantastic actor on stage. My sister did some acting as well. They were both were exceptionally talented and entertaining to watch.

I remember watching my brother and sister rehearse lines for plays they were in. My brother was so intense with every word he read. Even though I was around them a lot, I took a different road, sports. Little did I know, watching my brother on stage would prove to be beneficial in my undercover days and in prison.

The protective secret they kept from me, let me have a great childhood. They shielded me the horrors and details of my father's death. So, now for the rest of my life I will be my family's protector.

I later put the skills of my acting to the test when I kept the secrets of my police life at family dinners and gatherings. I would look into my mother's and siblings' eyes and tell them everything was good at work.

How the hell could I go to a big family reunion and tell my aunts and uncles what I did on the streets or what I had seen or done during my days on patrol and in plainclothes? How about this for a dinner conversation, "Hey, does anyone want to hear about a woman's eyes that had been pulled out from her eye sockets because her body was so decomposed?" or "Hey family, do you know what I saw this week? I had to watch a deviant bastard molest a two-year-old for ten minutes and deal crack out of his baby carriage before I could take him down." Or the intriguing stories of being shot at.

Not an ideal conversation to be having over dinner.

So I had to look everyone in their eyes and pull off the greatest acting job I could do and let them think I was safe. I had to keep my cop life and the dangers I faced every day on the streets a secret from them all.

But the performances were far from over. They continued in the visiting room while being incarcerated. My mother and sister would come twice a month sometimes bringing my little nieces. They would look at me and ask, "Are you okay, Pete?"

"Yes, all is good. I'm fine, please don't worry about me."

I guess they backed off a bit because I was in good shape. They knew I could handle myself if something went down, and I could. But the truth of the matter is, no person can fend off a pack of wolves. That's exactly what some inmates were, wolves. You're either an animal of prey or a wolf. I chose to be a lone wolf.

I remember one visit when my sister and mother came with my two nieces. My mother took the girls to the microwave to heat up some vending machine food. My sister knew something was wrong and asked, "Pete, what is going on with you? Please tell me, let me help you."

What the fuck could I say to her. "Hey, you know what I saw last night? I saw a guy get his skull caved in and his brains were all over the pavement. Then, I had an officer in the guard tower tell me if I moved, I would be shot in the back."

There was no way I was going to tell anyone, especially them, what was happening while I was incarcerated. They were my demons to carry alone. My family had a tough enough time carrying the weight of my conviction and incarceration. They didn't need any more stress in their lives.

The visiting room was always incredibly stressful for me and my family. It was great to see them every other week, but I knew what they had to endure before they got to sit at the table with me. The images of my family being frisked for weapons are burned in my brain forever, but that never stopped them from coming to see me.

During the visits, all prisoners from general population and protective custody were in the same room. That increased the danger levels tenfold. I had to have eyes in the back of my head. I was always ready to engage in combat if my family was in any type of danger.

Imagine all the general inmates licking their chops to attack an inmate in P.C. That was not a good decision the NYS prison system had in place. It is my understanding that the lawmakers of the correctional system have not changed it. It is just bat shit ludicrous.

Another reason I never let my family members know of the danger I was in during the visits was because the chances of running into an inmate I had once collared was greater during those times. My acting during my time in the street as a cop and while in prison had fooled my loved ones into thinking I was safe. Those were the secrets I would end up keeping from them for over two decades.

In my humble opinion, there is no real aspect of human

development when it comes to being incarcerated. The prisons are not there to help the inmates. Really, there are no resources for proper rehabilitation inside. It is up to the individual to decide how he will act when he finally obtains his freedom.

It is a known fact, through research done in California by Doctor Coyle, that eighty percent of men and women that have been in prison will go back within five years. While it might be just for that state, in my opinion, it also reflects New York state as well.

There is an old Hebrew proverb, "Remember those in chains, as if you were in chains."

I have only met a few correctional staff that really live by those words. The rest never think it could ever happen to them.

I once thought that way–how wrong I was. In a few seconds, my life changed dramatically. Prisons don't just lock you up, they lock you out from life.

The prison healthcare is also horrendous. Many prisoners have mental health problems, and they don't get the proper treatment for their varying illnesses. Several of the inmates shouldn't even be in prison but receiving help in mental facilities.

Prison itself creates mental problems for some men and women. Just being in solitary confinement for several months will begin to play tricks on one's mind. I was never in the hole, thank God. Imagine being in a concrete cell for twenty-three hours a day then put in a caged cell that is no bigger than five by ten feet for one hour. Most of the inmates will pace around the fencing like a caged animal. It's no wonder why convicts come out of prison eviller than when they went in.

When I was a cop, the confines of the 32nd precinct were deemed convict land. So many of the men who lived in that part of Harlem had done hard time in prison.

I remember an old-timer, also known as a dinosaur, once told me. "Pete, some of these guys get locked up on purpose to hone their skills inside. Prison is a school for some men to get better at the crimes they commit when they're released."

It is very unfortunate that they think this way. The main problem is when they get out of prison the convict has no money and no job. At times, even no home to go to. So, in some men's minds, they think, "Fuck it, I was getting three square meals a day and had a bed to sleep in. How am I going to make money? I have no other choice. I'll commit a crime. If I get caught, I go back inside and get a bed, my three hot meals back, and have no worries about the outside world."

I admit, when I got out, there were many times I thought of becoming a criminal. The main reason was that I couldn't get a job on the books. Those thoughts invaded my mind constantly, and almost won the battle. But I had and still have cop blood in me, and it will never leave me. In my heart and soul, good will always prevail.

CHAPTER TWELVE

While I was at Downstate, there were two Spanish brothers from East Harlem. The younger brother was Manuel, and the older brother was Reynaldo. In their heyday, they were considered two of the toughest men that controlled Lexington Avenue. They ran the operation known as the Bad Wolves out of the Jefferson houses.

Each member of the crew was required to live in that project. That was done to keep control of the gang and the stash houses. They controlled a large portion of the heroin that was being dealt in Spanish Harlem.

Both men never relied on a single foot soldier to enforce any type of punishment, be it a rival gang or one of their own, who might be skimming off the top of the proceeds. If anyone needed a beating or something worse, it was carried out by one of the brothers. The other crews in the area had given the brothers the nickname Double Trouble.

I had become friendly with Reynaldo while inside, he was an excellent handball player. The man had the craziest backspin when he served a handball. He was also a killer, and a family man.

During some of our conversations, he would hint that he'd seen me patrolling the Jefferson houses back in the late eighties when I was doing my field training. He was correct; I had seen him several times on the street giving his crew orders. When that subject came up, I always tried to avoid it by diverting to another topic.

Then there was times Reynaldo would tell me about some of his tactics when dealing with a rival gang. Other times, he would talk low and speak about how much of a bad ass his brother was. By Manuel's demeanor, I couldn't see the smaller man as a threat, but as the saying goes, never judge a book by its cover.

Reynaldo never directly came out and said who they had taken care of during their reign of power. He also never went into the details about what methods they used to enforce their punishment–he left that to my imagination, occasionally giving me a stone-cold wink. Let's just say I understood everything he was hinting at.

They were two merciless men you did not want on your bad side. His chilling stories were, at times, very disturbing to me. Especially, knowing the harm they could have brought down on my brothers in blue. He instilled fear into his crew and demanded they never disrespect 5-0, the police.

He explained to me, "My brother and I didn't want the extra heat on us. It's a hard-enough game out in the streets. So, why make it more difficult on my men."

When I heard the lives the two brothers led, it put in perspective how fucking wild the game I was involved as a lawman really was. During our talks, I made sure to keep the persona of not being phased by the malicious acts the brothers had carried out.

One day after a handball game, Reynaldo asked me, "Pete, did you train in your cell today? How about we do the card game Fit Deck during rec."

"Sounds good to me brother."

Fit Deck was a game we played doing pushups using poker cards. The numbered cards are the number of pushups we would do when flipped up. The face cards counted as ten, the aces were twenty-five, and the jokers counted as fifty. To make it more challenging, the person flipping the cards sometimes would flip three cards. Then, the other guy did the total that was called out. We knocked out three decks that night. I had already trained in the morning doing my ritual 1000 pushups. That day, I ended up doing 1800 pushups in total. Not a bad day of training.

After we had finished, there was still a half hour or so left to just sit and talk. First, Reynaldo and I checked on his brother, Manuel, who was sitting in a yellow chair watching TV. Reynaldo started to talk about their lives in the projects.

He then said to me, "Pete, I have to give it to you, most men would have offed themselves in here, in your position."

"Why do you say that brother?"

"You learned quickly to survive in this hell hole. You see no evil, you hear no evil, that's how you became one of us."

He had been correct. I had taught myself whatever the fuck I saw, I didn't see, and whatever I heard, I didn't hear. That was the only way I could make it out alive. The threat of violence was always in the air, every second of the day and night. That is the nature of the beast, called prison. I had trained myself never to let my guard down. Even while I slept, I was never fully asleep.

Reynaldo began to open-up and tell me what he and his brother were in for. Remember the golden rule, never ever ask someone, "What are you in for," unless they offer that information freely to you. Questions like that could get an inmate killed or even given a joker face with scars starting from the corners of their lips and ending at the ears.

Asking someone, "Did you, do it?" was the most asinine question to ask. Everybody claims they are innocent. The fact is, some really were, and the system incarcerated them on circumstantial evidence or false testimony. It's a common practice used in courts throughout the world. Listen, ninety percent of the inmates are guilty of the crimes they are in for, but that ten percent will plea out due to fear of being imprisoned for longer sentences.

Reynaldo began telling of the incident that took place the year before. The brothers had been devoted family men. Nothing, and I mean nothing, could separate them. They had made a vow to live hard and die together. Reynaldo told me that

Manuel and his wife had been in a rough patch in their marriage. The couple's relationship had been in trouble. He knew his wife was taking a ride on someone's else cock.

One night, the brothers told their wives they had business in New Jersey and wouldn't be home for the weekend. They had devised a plan of action and made the decision that the wife and her lover would be killed. The brothers had such an extensive pipeline of information on the streets that it only took a few hours to learn who the adulterer was. They had snared a trap for the man they had suspected of having the affair with Manuel's wife. It had been a rival gangs lieutenant from the East Side Crew.

That Saturday night, the men went over the details on how the execution would be carried out. Each brother carried a 9mm with a homemade suppressor attached to the barrel, and Manuel carried a machete. The brothers infiltrated his residence with such stealth that the wife and her lover never heard them enter the apartment.

They stood in the bedroom for several minutes watching them screw. That was done to fuel the brother's rage. Then, they opened fire on the adulterers filling them with bullets. After the smoke cleared from the air, Manuel took out the machete and hacked them up into pieces.

When the carnage was completed, the brothers exited the apartment. They took the stairs and ran to the rooftop of the building, escaping through an adjoining building's door, away from the crime scene. Reynaldo told me they had only gotten a few blocks before being captured by a passing patrol cruiser from the 23 pct. They weren't hard to notice, both men were covered in blood from head to toe.

The brothers had made a pact to go to prison together. Both Manuel and Reynaldo knew that going to trial was not an option. There was way too much evidence against them. So, both brothers pled guilty to murder in the second degree on two counts each. Life in prison with no possibility of parole.

They were both repeat offenders, and it was the three-strike rule against them. The one thing they had the lawyer get them in return for their plea, was they were to be put in the same prison.

While I listened to Reynaldo tell me the accounts of the gruesome murders, I noticed one of the inmates calling over to the guards. It was Manuel, his right arm and leg were shaking uncontrollably, but his left side was paralyzed. Tears were streaming down his left cheek; and his mouth was contorted. Reynaldo rushed over to his brother side trying to calm him down and assure him that he would be okay. Manuel had suffered a severe stroke. He was rushed over to the infirmary.

Days turned into weeks and there was still no sign of Manuel. Reynaldo's demeanor had taken a drastic turn for the worst. He was once again the ruthless gangster who had ruled the streets of Spanish Harlem. He would just give me a nod or a wave when we passed each other, nothing more. He no longer played handball with the other inmates. He was a ticking time bomb waiting to explode.

They transferred him out and sent him to a maximum prison a few weeks later. Both brothers were separated, never to see each other again. The only way they were able to respond to each other was through carefully monitored letters throughout the penal system.

CHAPTER THIRTEEN

I remember when I was finally granted my parole and sent home, away from my nightmare. The one question my friends would ask me, "So, Pete did you get sexually assaulted?"

My response was plain and simple, "No guys, I didn't get fucked nor did I fuck another inmate."

Before I went in, I made a solemn vow to myself. If anyone or any inmates tried that shit, I was ready to die before giving up my ass or mouth. I would die defending myself and take whoever with me that tried to commit any type of sexual deviant act against me. That was the one thing I would have killed or died for. My love for a women's body would never be tempted. The lack of sex with a female killed me inside, but I knew I wouldn't be inside forever. I'd be in the arms of a woman again soon.

To be honest, the lack of sex didn't affect me. I had other fucking things to worry about. The main thing on my mind was to stay alive and get home to my family. The other was not to get stabbed or mangled in that hell hole.

Well, the no-shanked part didn't work out, but at least it wasn't deep enough to kill me, it was more of a piecing. The inmates that are doing long bids want to give other inmates going away presents to remember their stay. There are many times they will stab, burn, or cut an inmate's face as a remembrance of where they came from.

When it comes to men or women that are incarcerated, there is one rule inside. You will either be the prey or the hunter when it comes to being raped or raping another prisoner. The perverted and deviant inmates don't care about how they get sex. It will be done by force or willingly. They will pick their marks the minute the new jailbait walks through the gates. They can smell the weakness on the men who won't fight back due to the fear of dying.

The facility which had become my final destination was designated for sexual predators on the outside. The men who raped and sodomized women and children. The sick motherfuckers who committed sexual acts on innocent human beings.

I knew Judge Allen had something to do with me being placed in Cayuga. What he didn't know was the vow I had made to myself and I was lucky enough to have derailed that bastards devious plan.

There are many inmates who have wives and children on the outside waiting for them to return home, but their need for physical affection and sex takes over. They seek comfort in another man's arms. I have no prejudice against the gay community or the men who engage in sex with each other while they are incarcerated. It just wasn't my thing.

Where I had been housed, there had been a couple who were cellmates together. One inmate, Damion, had a wife and son waiting for him on the outside. His cellmate, Frank, was openly gay. They had formed a union together and I guess that is how they were able to cope with being imprisoned.

I remember the first time I met Frank during an evening in the rec room. Frank and Damion were playing cards with a few other inmates. I asked to sit and watch the game and waited for a spot to open to get into the game. I already knew the other inmates except for the couple.

One of the other guys said, "Pete, the love birds holding hands are Damion and Frank."

Damion spoke first, he was a skinny, black guy. "Hey what's up bro?"

"How are you doing? Nice to meet you." Then I greeted Frank with a hello.

"Pete, please don't call me Frank. I go by the name Fran." He was a heavy-set white guy.

Holding back my smile and laughter, I said, "Sounds good, bud."

He shot me a crooked eyebrow like he was telling me, "That's madam to you." At least that is what I thought he was thinking.

Fran was a nice person who was in for drugs and larceny. His other half was more of a perp, Damion was a stone-cold gangster from Brooklyn. One night a group of us were taking our daily walk around the yard just shooting the shit.

I asked Damion, "Bro, how will you tell your lady that you were sleeping with another man?"

"I am not telling that bitch nothing. I know she's fucking one of my boys at home." "Fuck man, I'm sorry that she's stabbing you in the back."

"I knew that horny bitch wouldn't wait for me so, that's why I fuck Fran."

"What are you going to do with your home boy when you get home?"

"Well, you know I can't tell you that lawman. You're still a cop and I'm a gang banger." "Damion, I not a cop in here, I'm a fucking convict just like you and everyone else." "You still have cop blood in you right?"

"Fucking ay I do, and I will bleed blue forever, but I have lived on both sides of the fence. I'm one of you while I'm in here. That's the truth and law of the land, as far as I am concerned."

I remember one time we had been in lock down for a week straight. Shower time was kept to twice a week and no longer than ten minutes each. As I was drying off, Fran was next in line to take a shower. He had walked in before he should have, looking at my Johnson and upper body and said jokingly, "Hmm look what I have been missing all this time."

"Hey, Fran be a good girl and stop that freaky shit. I'm a

lady's man. No entrance here, bud." We had a good laugh at that.

My cellmate Mac and I would turn on our radio late at night and listen to the 1937 radio show The Shadow. The mysterious narrator of a radio program called Detective Story Hour. The character had the power to cloud men's minds so they couldn't see him. He was an expert detective who was highly trained in hand-to-hand combat. Also, a master of disguise. The people he helped in the series would be told they would be contacted when The Shadow needed them.

Before the show would begin, I would ask Mac, "Who knows what evil lurks in the hearts of men?"

Then he would snap off the quick response, "Only the Shadow knows."

That hour every night became our time to feel like cop's again–it was such a cool show.

On occasion we would hear Damion and Fran talking through vents, "Can you see the guards, D?"

"No, let's go."

"Oh, shit, Fran and Damion are at it again Mac."

We would be rolling on the floor cracking up. Then their bunk would start shaking and the moaning would begin. Luckily for us and the other inmates, it was over quickly. There were times a correction officer would be making their rounds and see them screwing.

"Hey, you two lovebirds knock that shit off now."

Being that I was in P.C., the sexual predators were placed in there for their own safety. If a deviant needed to be dealt with, which was 95 percent of the time, a Latin King or some other Latino gang would get into a fight in general population to get placed in P.C.. Or there were times they would lie and tell the C.O. they were scared for their life or being threatened just to get placed into P.C.. This was done for only one reason, to get to the sexual pervert and make them pay for their sins.

About a year into my bid, Officer Robinson from Z block called me downstairs. "Pete, you have a new arrival coming on your floor. Just stay clear of it. This inmate is nothing but a shit load of trouble waiting to happen."

"What do you mean by it?"

"He is a transgender."

"What is the inmates name?"

"Eric Valencia. He goes by the name Erica. You see Valencia, walk the other way. I'm telling you; a storm is coming."

"I'll let Mac know about the inmate coming to the floor when I get back to my cell. Thanks for the heads up."

"You're fucking hilarious, heads up. Pete, you said 'head'."

We started cracking up.

"Robinson you are sick man you know that."

"Why thank you, sir."

When I got back into the cell, I went to tell Mac that Valencia was coming to the block. "Hey brother, Robinson told me we have a transgender coming to the block."

"Yesterday's news Pete the inmate is up here in a holding cell waiting to be bunked with someone."

"Did you get a look at the new inmate, bro?"

"Yes, Valencia is Mexican and has a nice set of tits. It fucking freaked me out, bro."

"Hey, Mac don't get any funny ideas, or I will tell your girl."

We started laughing. "It's just strange to see a dude walking around with a rack."

"Why, you never saw them on the street turning tricks?"

"No, not up in New Rochelle."

"Shit, brother, they are all over Times Square. There is a shit load of them up in Harlem turning tricks. They even have pimps. They give blowjobs for five bucks. I would catch a John when I was in my cruiser canvassing the area of 125th to 132nd Street along Park Avenue. Then I would pull the guy over and ask him, 'You know that's not a chick, right?' Most of those Johns couldn't tell it was a guy looking to blow them. My line to them was, 'Hey jerky if you don't want your dick to fall and get sucked off by a man, get the fuck out of here. Don't come back, go home to your wife and kids.'"

To be honest, I never understood how they didn't recognize that they were men pretending to be women. I know that transgenders believe they are women and there is nothing wrong with that. I don't have anything against them at all. But the Johns should have been able to spot their Adams apple and deep voice when negotiating what service, they wanted.

Our cell door opened for rec that night. Several inmates rushed by us to get seats in the rec room. They were all cleaned up like they were going out on a date. Looking their best for the new girl on the block.

"What the fuck, Mac? Are these crazy bastards for real, they're that hard up?"

"Hey brother they need some loving. They are trying to get Valencia to bunk with them." Finally, the new inmate came into the rec room and each inmate had fire in his eyes. All I heard was whistling and them throwing comments at Valencia. Each convict tried his best to win the heart of the transgender. I got up to get a drink and as I passed Valencia, he cooed at me.

I turned around and said, "Knock that shit off asshole, I'm fucking straight."

"Well my name is Erica and you never know big boy."

"Hey, Eric keep to your side of the room and find an inmate who wants to be with you."

"That's not my name, call me Erica."

"Sure, thing Eric."

The new inmate was told to report to cell nineteen. Little did he know who, or what was his new cellmate. The fill-in guards had paired him with the deadly Latin King, Wilder, who had caved the other Spanish inmates head in while we were in the yard a few months earlier. Wilder kept to himself. He chose to stay inside his cell away from the other inmates. I guess that was better for all of us.

The new inmate was told to report to his new cell. I looked at Mac and the other prisoners who had tried in vain to be paired up with Valencia.

I said in a low voice, "Are they fucking out of their minds putting him in there with Wilder? He'll tear him to shreds."

The officers on duty that night was not the regular crew. How the hell didn't they read Wilder's jacket? The guy was a stone-cold killer and rapist. Later, we headed back to the cell Mac turned on the radio and we waited for The Shadow to come on.

The guard yelled out, "Lights out convicts, keep it down and go to sleep."

The program was about halfway through when we heard smashing in one of the cells. It was bad, someone was catching a brutal ass beating. Then we heard the inmate screaming through the floor vent, "Help me, he's raping me. Help please, he's going to kill me." It was Valencia screaming for his life. Then, we heard a loud grunt come through the vent. Wilder had finished brutally raping the transgender.

The guards took their time getting to cell where the violent sexual assault and beating was occurring. Wilder was a bloody mess, none of the blood was his. His boxer shorts were covered in feces and blood. They threw him to the ground, restrained the hitman and dragged him out of the cell. Immediately, they called for the orange crush to respond forthwith to the bloody rape scene.

Valencia was half beaten to death with a broken arm, ribs, nose, and his orbital socket was crushed. He also suffered a fractured skull.

We later found out that Eric/Erica was sitting on the toilet going to the bathroom. While she was taking a crap, Wilder had caught a glimpse of the inmate's fake tits and got turned on and just went crazy, beating the poor bastard to a pulp while sodomizing him. Valencia never returned to the cell block and Wilder was transferred to a Maximum facility.

Prison makes men and women do things they would never do on the outside world.

While incarcerated you're stripped of your clothes and possessions. You're given prison issued clothes and toiletries. Not only is the inmate stripped of their belongings, but they're also stripped of their pride. I personally knew I would have to be mentally and physically stronger than any other inmate. Otherwise, I would not make it out to see my family. The other side of the coin was, if I didn't stay focused and have hope for a future on the outside, I would emotionally be screwed up for rest of my life. I chose to survive and take back my life as best as I could.

Time would become my enemy while being incarcerated. Minutes became hours. Days became months. There were times I felt like I was in the Twilight Zone. I later would become an expert in counting hours of the days that I had left inside. Especially when I had to deal with an inmate or correction officer I disliked.

I would tell myself, "Okay Pete, you only have 90 days left to deal with this guy. You only have to deal with this asshole for a few hundred more hours of your life, and you will never see these pieces of shit or place again."

CHAPTER FOURTEEN

There are people in this world that will say things just to get a rise out of you. I learned while I was on patrol that there were gang members that would challenge me verbally to try and intimidate me. They wanted cops to fear them and their gang.

They'd often say, "You don't respect them."

Or something like, "If you didn't have that badge and gun, I would kick your fucking ass."

Sometimes I'd get pissed off and unbuckle my gun belt and say, "Now I am not a cop let's do this."

I didn't do this to be a bad ass, I did it to make a point. "It isn't respect, you're looking for, you want to instill fear in people. Respect is earned, not a given right to anyone."

That would usually defuse the situation. If a police officer, or anyone for that matter, shows fear then they become the prey.

Then, there are those people who say something crazy and carry out the threats they've spoken. These are the most dangerous individuals that walk the earth. They have no morals or conscience and will carry out among the worst criminal acts on society.

During my time on the force and while I was incarcerated, I stood face to face with these hardened criminals. I needed to pull off the greatest undercover role I would ever be faced with. I had to prove that I was indeed one of them and not on the side of the law. I formed bonds with inmates that were in gangs, murderers, and convicts who were the most violent people in New York.

The only inmates that I wouldn't speak with were the men who were convicted of sexual crimes. My final penitentiary was a prison for those scumbags that housed forty percent of them. But I stayed clear of those predators and so did the Latino gang members–they would target these types of convicts. To be very honest, I had no problem staying clearing of them and wanted every sexual predator to rot in hell.

I met Blanco, the Neta king, while I was at Rikers. We had long conversations about our lives on both sides of the fence. I made sure to always be careful about the war stories that I relayed to him. If I said too much or spoke in depth about an arrest, it could have been a perp he may have known, and that would have presented a huge problem for me.

Yes, we were both in prison but make no mistake, we were on opposite sides of the law. Blanco was a man of power on the streets of Manhattan, but he held even more power inside the New York state prison system. He was the top boss in the Neta organization.

Blanco told me the history of his organization. "They were founded by Carlos Torres also known as 'La Sombra' (The Shadow). It began in the seventies when some pro-independence political prisoners were in the maximum prison called Oso Blanco." I had to smile when he told me that.

"Is that a coincidence that your last name is Blanco?" We had a good laugh at that.

These men had formed a mutual protection group to protect and defend inmates from the abuses committed by the guards, as well fight the prison gang 'G'27' also known to them as the insects. The G'27 called the Neta's worms.

By the eighties, the Neta's had become the most powerful gang in the prison and a majority of the inmates became loyal to the Neta's. But the leader of the G'27 wouldn't back down, so with the help of paid off authorities, he plotted the assassination of the Neta leader.

They were able to ambush him when he was out of reach from his soldiers and the watchful eyes of the Neta gang. The Neta's are extremely religious and always attended the chapel to pray. That's where the G'27' gang attacked the leader of the Neta gang when he left the service. He was brutally stabbed and shot in the stomach by a 38 pistol which was more than likely smuggled in by a corrupt guard.

During the investigation, the prison authorities learned that it had been an inside job within the Neta organization itself. Some of the Neta lieutenants had been at odds with their leader and wanted to go into the business of drug trafficking in the prison system and on the streets.

The loyal members of the Neta leader exploded throughout the prison and took over several wings of the prison facility. They showed their power with violent and brutal force with retaliation against the G'27 gang. Their main target was the leader of the G'27 gang. The Neta's dug and chiseled their way through the walls of the prison using kitchen utensils and their bare hands. Finally reaching the cell of the G'27 leader, they held him down and the loyal members of the Neta gang stabbed him over one hundred and fifty times and cut him into eighty-four pieces.

They supposedly mailed certain body parts to a few people of interest. The mother received her son's detached finger. They sent an ankle and foot to the warden of the prison to show they were in control of the facility. They even delivered the eyes of the dead G'27 leader to his former second in command.

In the years that followed, the Neta organization took over prisons throughout the U.S and other countries. By the late eighties, the Neta became an association and is also known as "Holy Death".

Their rivals vary throughout territories–the Crips, (DDP) Dominicans Don't Play, MS-13 and lifelong sworn enemy G'27 (Grupo27). Late in the nineties, the Bloods also became a sworn enemy to the Neta gang.

I had become fascinated with the history of the gang. They wear rosary beads around their necks and dress in white clothes which is part of the gang's identity.

Blanco and I had formed such a tight bond that at one

point I sent someone to check on his child while she was in the hospital with a broken eardrum. Eventually before I had left Rikers, he informed me that I was to be an honorary member in the Neta's. I explained in a very polite manner that I couldn't accept his offer.

He understood but also let me know, "The Neta's have your back while you are inside. You are a man of honor and loyalty."

The main reason for this was that I hadn't sold out my brothers in blue for a gold shield and my potential freedom. I had earned their respect. They didn't view me as a cop inside the prison walls, I was one of them–at least I appeared to be one of them. Several times, while I was at Downstate and Cayuga, I'd get a nod from a Neta member.

"Blanco sends his regards."

Along with Blanco, I had become somewhat of a father figure to an inmate named Country, who was from North Carolina. He was persuaded by a friend from his last foster home to move to New York when he turned eighteen. The day he became of age, he took a bus to New York. He was given directions to his friend's house where his life of crime began the very next day. Country was a top-notch auto mechanic and knew any car inside and out. The two friends started off small by jacking cars late night on the streets of Brooklyn. Their main area at first was Park Slope and Marine Park.

The reputation of the two car thieves spread throughout Brooklyn and several chop shops were looking for their services. The two became four which then grew to an eight-man crew. They were stealing anywhere between ten to twenty cars a week.

Country had taken the reins of the crew and became the shot caller. They had caught the eye of a garage owner who specialized in expensive sports cars. Their new acquaintance wasn't exactly a made guy, but he was high in the food chain with one of the five families. Country was smart enough not to ask his new partner who he worked for. All he cared about was making a shit load of money.

Country's mistake had been his own greed. He was rolling in dough, but it was never enough for the young man. One night, he and his crew went for their biggest score and tried to rip off a fully loaded eighteen-wheeler car carrier. The truck was carrying multiple 1996 Mercedes Benzes. That was his last night of freedom for the next six years.

He told me one night, "Pete, I don't know my mother or father or if I ever had any siblings." He had been abandoned as a small child and never forgave his blood parents for leaving him.

"I'm sorry my friend, that's horrible. Listen, I never met my blood father either."

"Yeah but you had your mother, brother, and sister, right?"

"Yes, bud, I did have that, and I'm a very lucky man to have them in my life."

I saw the glazed look in the man's eyes, he wanted to burst out in tears, but that was never going to happen, at least not in front of me.

Country was leader in the dorm and the black inmates did what he commanded them to do. The house was under Blanco and Country's control.

Surprisingly, the two inmates who would be sworn enemies on the street, kept peace within the house. They would sit at a table with their second in command standing behind them. If there was beef between two inmates, they would decide who was right and who would be punished. No inmate dared to challenge these two men or their decisions on the matter presented before them.

One afternoon, the two leaders sat at the table for an hour planning a hit on someone. All I kept thinking was, I hope they aren't going to kill someone. I was leaving the next day to my next destination, Downstate. I didn't need any type of trouble before I was to leave Rikers.

Night fell upon the house quickly and I was given instructions to stay on my cot and not join in on the "meet and greet" Blanco called the gauntlet. I witnessed one of the most brutal beatings I'd ever seen and heard a vicious sodomy of a sexual deviant who preyed on a young girl.

The two leaders enforced their own laws and the prisoner's brand of justice. They were the law, Judge, and executioner if need be.

If an inmate has broken any of the implicit rules of prison on the inside or the outside, that person is dealt with while being incarcerated. In my opinion, if you ask any of the Latino inmates who would they rather be incarcerated with, a sexual deviant or a cop, the cop will win that vote hands down.

CHAPTER FIFTEEN

During evening rec hours, my time was spent playing cards for cigarettes, watching TV, and talking with other inmates, some of whom I became somewhat friendly with. There had been only one person I fully trusted, however, and that was Mac, my cellmate. I guess it was a code I lived by. A brother in blue was just that, a brother to me. It never mattered and still doesn't.

"My brothers and sisters in blue throughout the world are my extended family."

When one of them dies in the line of duty or is harmed in anyway, a jolt of pain goes through my entire body. The pain I feel in my heart and soul is the feeling that I failed all of them because I had been incarcerated. Everything I had fought for in the streets to make the city a safer place to live, had backfired on me in the worst of ways. There is no one to blame but myself.

Yes, the deck was stacked against me when it pertained to the judicial system, but it was my obsession for a detective shield that ended my career.

One of the things that always fascinated me was hearing how the most violent criminals on the block ended up inside. I never asked why unless they asked me first. Then, the criminal war gates of hell opened for me. Believe me, I was not shy about learning what was inside the minds of those sick bastards.

There was one inmate who was quiet and kept to himself. He was a white guy in his mid-forties. The other inmates gave him a nickname, which no one had the balls to call him to his face, Ivan the cannibal.

One night, I decided to offer Ivan a cigarette, and he was thankful for the smoke. After shooting the shit, he looked up at me and asked, "Why did your job fuck you over like they did?"

"Ivan, I made some enemies who were high ranking bosses. I fuck around too much with the cops who investigate the police."

"But did you commit the crimes they convicted you of?"

"Well let's put it this way bud, I never robbed anyone or stole evidence. As for the falsifying business records. I never wrote any reports that weren't true to the best of my knowledge. The problem is, a cop must keep a detailed log of his movements every half hour or so, it's called a memo book. There were times I would put myself somewhere in a project doing a building vertical, but I was actually in another area doing some type of recon watching drug crews on the street clocking."

"What is clocking, Pete?"

"That's just a slang word for dealing drugs, bud. So, I guess I am guilty of that. To be honest with you, I don't know any cop on patrol that's not done that some time in their career. That's my story Ivan."

"They put you in here with us for that bullshit?"

"Yes, when you piss off the wrong people who hold power, they fuck you right in the ass. So, what's your story and please don't hold back on any of the details."

"Couldn't you have reported any other cops doing stuff that was illegal?"

"Ivan, I live by a code called the Blue Wall of Silence. I'll leave it at that. To me, loyalty to my blood family and my brothers in blue is the most important thing in my life."

"But that silence and loyalty cost you your freedom. Why would you do that if you could be free and not be in here with us?"

"Would you sell out your brother, sister or any person who had your back in a war just to keep your job and be free? I couldn't throw any of my brothers and sisters under the bus and I never would. They have families too; you know what I mean?"

"Pete, what do you mean by war, you weren't in the

military?"

"I am talking about the war on drugs, Ivan. It's all around us, even in this hell hole. So, tell me your story now, Ivan."

"I'll tell you, but you must keep this between us and never tell the other inmates. I like my reputation in here as Ivan the cannibal."

"My lips are sealed, my friend. I will not speak to anyone about what we speak about tonight."

"Well, I'm sure you heard that I committed cannibalism, right? Or something to that effect."

I just nodded in his direction.

"I was a worker in a small construction company. One day I made the mistake of having my now deceased wife pick me up after work. From that day on she would always offer to take me to and pick me up from my job.

"She started wearing makeup and was constantly worrying about her weight and appearance. She really was looking hot, and I thought she was doing it all for me. Our marriage was kind of in turmoil. I thought the filthy bitch was trying to rekindle the flame with me. I hadn't fucked her in months. We weren't doing anything sex wise while she was making herself look good. I started to notice she was talking with someone on the phone late at night when she thought I was asleep. That's when I became suspicious of her being unfaithful to me. When the phone bill finally came, I checked it for the number she was talking with. Sure, enough a number from another area code showed up on the bill several times. I looked up the area code, it was from New Jersey. She was either calling the number or receiving calls from that person. It was a lot of calls, Pete. I just didn't have any idea who the fuck it was.

"There had been only one thing on my mind. I was going to hunt him down and kill the bastard. I know what you are thinking, Pete. My wife was just as guilty. Once I had the proof, I would deal with her too. I vowed to make them both pay with their lives. Something had changed in me when I discovered her infidelity. I became a dark and twisted man and I embraced it. During that time, I would look at her, and just saw a filthy cheating slut. I just waited and plotted my revenge.

"Several months later I walked into my boss's office to ask him a question. He was speaking to someone on the phone. I had interrupted him speaking very provocatively to a woman on the other end. That's when I recognized my wife's voice clear as day on the other end of the conversation. I knew that sound in her voice, she was playing with herself, moaning and breathing heavily. He quickly cupped his hand over the receiver to muffle her voice. He answered my question quickly to get me the hell out of his office. At that moment, I started to visualize how I would kill them both. After he provided me with the answer to my question, I left his office smiling. Now I knew who she was sleeping with."

While I listened to Ivan, I began to put myself into his mind. I wanted to see through the eyes of the executioner and place myself at the murder scenes.

"Pete the fucking rage inside me took over. She picked me up after work, right on time and we went home, not speaking a word to each other. I cleaned up, and she announced supper was ready. Her biggest mistake that day was making a roast that needed to be sliced, with a nice sharp butcher knife."

Ivan then sucked in with his mouth making his tongue hit the roof of his mouth before smiling at me. The fucking sound was so unnerving.

"She handed me the butcher knife, and I sliced the meat slowly. I ran the blade down the roast and listened to the sound the meat made as I cut it. I watched how it slowly tore away and fell onto the wooden cutting board and how the blood from the meat formed a little puddle on it.

"I began to fantasize that I was peeling her flesh from her body. After I finished slicing the meat from her and letting the fantasy play out in my head, I served her a few pieces of meat nice and rare." He gave me a bone chilling wink.

At that moment I was able to put myself in that kitchen with Ivan. It was as if I was standing next to him.

"I went back to the carving board, cutting two more pieces for myself. I licked the blood off the butcher's knife and let the animal blood drip out of my mouth to the corners.

"I slowly started creeping up behind her. I took hold of the back of her head and grabbed her hair and yanked her head back. Her eyes widened as she was staring at the ceiling. Then I slowly slit that bitches throat from ear to ear. The sound of her gurgling as I let her bleed out was such a blissful moment for me. In all honesty. I tried to decapitate her. I made sure I cut through her vocal cords so she couldn't scream.

"After that, I started stabbing her for all the times she had fucked him. What a beautiful sound a sharp knife makes when it is plunged into a human being. It is like a swishing sound. Unless the blade hits a bone, then you will hear a cracking sound along with swishing sounds. I let her head slam onto the kitchen table and left her there in the kitchen. I showered and watched her blood run off my hands and arms into the drain making a circular pattern. I dressed quickly and headed back to work.

"I was driving like a mad man ignoring the lights and any traffic laws. Luckily, no cops were around at that time. I knew he would be finishing his paperwork during those hours. He always waited for the shift to end before closing out the invoices of the day's work.

The butcher's knife was tucked behind the small of my back under my belt. I startled him as I walked through the door. My boss turned white as a ghost when he saw me standing there. His guilty eyes began to water in fear, and he was stuttering asking me, "What are you doing here Ivan? It is late, I thought you punched out an hour and half ago.'"

"Oh, I think we both know why I am here Tom, you wife stealing motherfucker. It is time for you to answer for your crimes." He reached for the phone to call 911. Then I grabbed his hand and smashed it onto the table, so he'd release the phone. Once he opened his hand to release the phone receiver, I held it down and stuck the knife into his hand pinning it into the wooden desk. After a minute of him screaming, I freed the blade just enough from the wood, but left the blade lodged in his hand, then I cut it apart."

Ivan Smiled, and he said, "He looked like a true Star Trek fan. You know how Spock greeted people with his fingers in the V shape."

Then without missing a beat into his diabolical story, he went on describing the gruesome murder of his boss. "I swung the blade across his neck. I tried to decapitate that fucking scumbag cheating bastard, but it was too much trouble to take his head from his body.

"After watching the blood pour from his neck onto his desk for several moments, I just started stabbing him over and over until I was too tired to run the blade into him anymore. I sat in a chair on the opposite side of his desk for a while just looking at him, but my thirst for his blood wasn't fulfilled. That is when I decided to cut a few of his fingers off along with his tongue and cock. I decided to consume his tongue and fingers. I stuck his penis in his mouth. I had never eaten human flesh before. I thought to myself, 'How bad can it taste? There is always a first for everything, right?' He had a stove in his office where he would cook for himself. I grabbed one of those old fashion black frying pans and melted some butter and sprinkled some salt and pepper in the pan, then fried his fingers and tongue up. To be honest, it didn't taste that bad. It was a little difficult to eat his tongue, it was very tough and chewy."

Breaking him from his horrendous thoughts, I cracked a joke. "Hey Ivan, remind me never to get stranded on an island with you."

I just sat there taking it all in and kept studying the ruthless killer convict. There was pure evil and enjoyment in his eyes as he explained the murders. I tried to bring Ivan back to reality, separating him from the demon that had possessed him throughout the retelling of the murders.

He then said, "I want to thank you for letting me get that off my chest. I haven't spoken about the incident in over a decade. I needed to release it from my mind."

"You're welcome, Ivan."

I tried to make him laugh by saying, "Remind me never to eat chicken fingers around you."

His stare took a quick turn which froze me for a second. I thought to myself, Fuck, Pete you just crossed the line with him. But then he began laughing uncontrollably.

"You are a funny guy. I needed a laugh like that."

The guard yelled out, "Time to lock in, convicts."

"Have a good night, Ivan. Talk to you tomorrow."

I went back into my cell with the strangest feeling. It felt like my mind have been invaded by one of the evilest deranged human beings I had ever encountered. The way he described the killings was just terrifying. But in turn, that is what drew me into that kind of violent world for nearly a decade. I realized these men are the worst of the worst. The thing that bothered me most was I was in with them.

Why the fuck, weren't these violent inmates kept in maximum prisons? The answer was simple. They had already done a lot of their bids in maxes and kept out of trouble. That is the way their statuses got changed. They were rewarded for being well behaved and staying out of trouble. Then, the violent offender is dropped down to medium facilities. Real nice, put the inmate who was in for a bullshit a non-violent felony beside the rapists and murderers. The system is just fucking insane.

There was a white inmate who had long black hair, a mustache, and a beard. He wasn't a tall fellow. He stood around five feet and had sleeve tattoos. The black and Latino inmates called him the Hick from Upstate New York. The man was a superb artist. He would always be in the rec room with drawing paper and colored pastels, which he likely got his family or a friend to purchase from a professional art store.

The pictures the inmate drew were simply amazing to the eye. I'm not an art person of any sort, but this guy could bring any picture to life. His deal was any inmate could ask for a picture of their loved ones and he would draw it up for them in exchange for the cigarettes. He was able to keep himself well stocked in smokes.

I hadn't been present for my youngest child's birth. Not being there for that occasion was tearing me apart. It was bad enough not to be around for my two other children, but the absence of witnessing my youngest son being born destroyed me.

I had a nice picture of him as a baby and wanted the Hick to do a portrait. One night during rec, I sat across from him as he was completing the finishing touches of someone's lady. It was a bit provocative but pleasant to look at. He brought every curve and line of the woman's body to life. Her eyes could follow you around the room, their depth was insurmountable.

I waited for him to finish what he was doing before asking him, "How are you doing tonight, bud?"

"You know I have a first name, Buddy."

"Sorry man, I really don't know your name. I apologize."

"No biggie, my name is Brad."

"I'm Pete, it's nice to meet you." I pulled out the photo of my son and showed it to him. "How much to do this portrait?"

"Two cartons of smokes, that is what I charge for my work."

"Okay cool, how about I give you one carton now and the other after it's finished."

"Sounds like a deal. Go get me the smokes and I'll start it tonight and have it done by Sunday before evening rec starts."

I went back to my cell and grabbed a carton of Marlboro menthol smokes and handed them to Brad. "Alright see you Sunday, Pete."

Sunday night came, and he took the portrait out from an oak tag folder. It was amazing, the drawing looked better than the actual photo. He made my son's eyes look like they were real–I stared at the picture waiting for the eyes to blink back at me.

I had no words for the man. "Brad this is truly incredible, thank you so much."

"It's my pleasure. This is what I love to do in here. It gives me a purpose and I can help other inmates. Plus, it kills time in this shit hole. Without my drawings, I would kill someone in here." That statement took me by surprise.

At the time, I had no idea what he was in for. I had also noticed he never drew any portraits for any of the black inmates. That struck me as odd, but I kept that to myself.

"Hey, do you want to see my ink on my back?"

"I guess so. Sure, show it to me."

As he rolled up his shirt, he looked around the room to make sure none of the black or Latino inmates were looking in our direction. Then, I saw one of the craziest things I 'd ever witnessed in my life. His entire back was the confederate flag. He pulled his shirt back down.

"How you like that? You didn't know I am part of a white supremacist group, did you?"

"Well no, I didn't Brad. Honestly, I thought you were a biker either from the Hell's Angels or the Pagans Motorcycle Club."

"Nay, I know plenty of those dudes, but I just believe in white power. I believe we are supreme. No worries, your safe with me, Pete."

"I am glad to hear that Brad, thanks."

At that moment I was kind of pissed that I let him draw the portrait. I was thinking to myself, Motherfucker, I could snap your neck in a second if I wanted to, or better yet, rip your spine through your chest cavity. It was times like that when I felt I was one of them. A convict–evil. Brad snapped back at me.

"I already know why you're in here. You were a dirty cop, right?"

I ground my teeth and felt my jaw muscles bulging from my jaw line.

"No bud, I was doing my job and got screwed over."

"Yeah, that is what we all say in the joint. We all got fucked over by the system and the pigs. No offense, Pete."

"None taken, Brad. So, what are you in for?"

"Well, I am serving twenty to life for killing a nigger."

"Fuck man, you trying to get us killed in here. Keep that shit to yourself and lower your fucking voice."

"Sorry man, I just hate them. If you aren't white, you aren't right. So, let me tell you what got me thrown in here with these fuckers. I lived up in Orange County where we have a compound and hold meetings. Our organization is just waiting for the right time. So, my white brothers train and shoot shit up. It's there where we would bring one of them and fuck them up."

"What do you mean? You go out and stalk black people."

"No, if they happen to venture into the neighborhood or a connecting town, we deal with them."

Do I really want to hear this scumbag's story of how he committed murder? Brad continued.

"One night we were in our local bar pulling back shots of whiskey and drinking beer. We were also snorting a shit load of coke and were completely plastered. Then, in steps a man of color. Is that the correct way of saying negro?"

I just stayed quiet waiting for him to continue.

"We let the man order his drink. He had ordered a shot of Hennessey. The president of my chapter put his arm around my shoulder and said, 'That will be the last shot that fucking bastard will feel slide down his throat. Is that understood, brother?'

"I stepped over to the guy and said to him, 'You must be lost boy'. He responded with a smart-ass remark, "Listen shorty, I just want to have a few drinks and I will be on my way." "A few seconds later we were beating the living shit out of him with whatever we could get our hands on. Pool sticks, pool balls wrapped in bandanas, smashing beer bottles over his head and against his face."

As he began to describe the brutal assault, I imagined myself in the bar sitting on a bar stool drinking some shots of whiskey or Jägermeister. I visualize the white supremacist group breaking the pool cues over the man's head. I could see them wrapping the pool balls in their bandanas. I heard the man's head being caved in with the crushing blows he was receiving from the violent gang.

Then Brad pulled me out of my thoughts telling more of the brutal assault, "I stabbed him several times with a broken beer bottle. The sound of a broken beer bottle entering human flesh is so exhilarating. It's a ripping sound like when you put a shovel into the ground or sand."

I pictured the victim being repeatably stabbed and cut by those savages–fucking low lives.

"We made him into a human piñata. The boys tied his hands and feet together with rope and stripped him of his clothes. Don't worry, we let him keep his underwear on."

"That was pretty white of you to do."

Brad snapped me a looked. I wanted that little shithead to make a move on me. I had played it out in my mind of how I would smash my head into the bridge of his nose until it shattered or until one of us passed out from the blows of our heads colliding.

He continued with the story. "We bound him to the rear fender of my pickup truck. Man, that boy had some kick in him. He just kept fighting for his life and his freedom."

"What else did you expect him to do, Brad? Just lay there and let you and your gang kill him without fighting back?"

He looked at me as if I were sticking up for his victim–which I was. It didn't matter the color of his skin; I would have felt that anger for any person's life.

"Here comes the good part. Now that we had him hooked up to the rear fender of my truck." I closed my eyes needing to see and feel what that monster felt during those critical moments of his murderous life. "I dragged his ass around the bar's dirt parking lot. Doing donuts with my truck. He was screaming at first and begging me to stop. My crew was cheering and yelling for me to go faster. His body was spinning like a top. I stopped my truck and let the cloud of dirt that filled the air clear. I yelled out to the boys, 'Put a beer on ice and have some lines of snow ready for me. I will be back in a few minutes.'

"Then, I sped off onto the highway. I rolled down my window so I could hear him screaming and begging for his life. It was music to my ears, his whaling. I just put the petal to the metal and went faster. Then, there were no more pleas for his life. I couldn't hear anymore cries or moans from the injuries he had sustained. I got out of my pickup truck to check on him. He was a bloody mess. The skin from his torso and legs were ripped off while some stayed attached to his body. He was still breathing very shallow.

"I yelled at him, 'Well boy, let me finish you off with a good ole white lighting drag.' So I hit the gas petal and drove another thousand yards and slammed on the brakes. I heard his body hit the back tires, so I rolled over him for good measure. I stepped out from my truck and saw he was finally dead as a door nail. After that, I cut him loose and rolled his body to the side of the road and threw him into a ditch.

"I went back into my truck feeling fulfilled that I had done the chapter proud. I drove as fast as I could back to the bar to have a celebration drink. The boys wanted to know what he had looked like and how long he lasted during the ride.

"I said, 'Now gentleman, you know I don't kiss and tell. If you want to see his body, drive down the road a few miles until you see my trucks skid marks from slamming on my brakes.' We partied until closing time. I drove right past the troopers who had covered the body in a white sheet. I was so fucked up that night, that I didn't realize there were cars passing me on the opposite side of the road. They saw that I was dragging a body from the back of my truck. Some good citizen jotted down the make and year of my truck and gave it to the state troopers.

"The next morning my door was kicked in by a squad of troopers and town cops. One of them held a pumped shotgun to my head and yelled, 'Give me a fucking reason to blast your head from your shoulders.'

"I took it to trial and lost. They hit me with twenty to life. None of the chapter members attended my trial, but they do look out for my family because I kept silent. I have already completed ten years in prison. Now, I just keep to myself and do my drawings."

"Well, that is one fucked up story, Brad, if I was you, don't let them see your back. And don't fuck with any of them. White inmates are the minority in here, which I think your aware of."

"Yeah, that is why I keep to myself."

CHAPTER SIXTEEN

The one thing all men and women who have been in prison agree on is that there are two significant days of the incarceration process. The first is when you step inside the prison gates.

When I first stepped through the gates of hell, I knew there was a chance I may never again see the outside world. I can remember so vividly the guard's keys entering the lock and turning the tumbler and hearing that loud locking sound of the gate sealing me away from freedom. I can still hear and feel my heart dropping and my soul leaving my body. It was as if I had lost all my humanity. The glory I had once felt while being a defender for the greatest city in the world, had been ripped from me. My journey began as a silent purgatory and would continue for two years.

The second most important day of an inmate's life while being incarcerated, is when they are released. I remember the weeks, days, and hours that led up to my release date. It felt like an eternity.

So many questions ran through my mind, but one stood out, "How could an ex-police officer who was now an ex con fit into society?"

One day in addiction group, the counselor wanted us to speak about our first twenty-four hours in prison and then speak on what we expected of our last day of being incarcerated.

Some of the inmates just said, "We aren't getting out any time soon, so it's fruitless to talk about that."

One hard nose inmate said, "How the fuck, do you think we're going to feel about our release date? Shit, it will be like orgasming a hundred times inside your lady love."

"Okay then, share what you all experienced on your first day."

After the group had finished reflecting on what they'd gone through their first day, I realized some of those guys went through pure hell. Two inmates had the shit kicked out of them in the bullpen, which is the holding cell and also known as the tank. I'd been lucky enough to be in a holding cell alone. Well, maybe not that lucky.

The thoughts that had raced through my mind during the first twenty-four hours were horrific. There is an old saying, "The mind is a beautiful thing to waste." The mind is and will always be an inmate's worst and greatest foe and adversary. Until I was able to control my mind, it was by far the worst enemy I had ever encountered.

The hours that led up to my final days in prison were tense and uneasy. I kept questioning myself. How am I going to adjust to this new life as a citizen, not a lawman? What type of father will I be to my three small children? How will I protect them? How will I function in the world? Will I be able to get employment? How will my family and friends look at me now? Would they think of me as the cop I once was or the convict who was returning from prison?

I knew in my heart that my mother, my siblings, and my blood relatives would accept me as the same me I always had been to them. Not one of them ever judged me for what had happened. But regardless, I felt as though I had failed all of them.

I will say this, those were some of the scariest hours that I have ever counted down.

That night after the rec session, Mac and I were waiting for The Shadow to come on. When the radio show ended, we started to speak about our court cases. Mac took a deep drag on his cigarette letting the smoke drift out of his mouth.

As smoke traveled across the room, he said, "Its war story time, Pete, you go first. My arrests aren't as action packed as yours. Tell me about one of the drug crews you went after."

"Alright, sounds good, brother. There was this gang called Obsession that operated out of the Wagner houses. They were clocking. That crew was out there 365 days a year. The dealers were paid double time on holidays. Crazy, right, brother? The leader of the crew was a mutt named Bob Nelson who was partners with a drug kingpin named George who controlled most of the Bronx's heroin trade.

"This crew dealt their heroin in vials instead of packing it in the normal wax paper. The vials had 'Obsession' written on them. Bob controlled the Wagner houses at first, slinging crack cocaine. The Manhattan crew trademark for the crack, was pink top vials. I focused my attention on them for several months. The main problem I ran into was, there were no buildings to do my recon from. Nelson made sure that the dealers were pitching inside the hallways and lobbies of the project. The buildings they used also had a front entrance door that led to the lobbies and rear exit door. That created major problems for me and any other cops trying to catch the Obsession gang.

"Whenever my partner and I were investigating them, we had to always call for an additional unit to cover one of the exits. I was still in uniform, so it was difficult to go unnoticed when we would enter the building. My squad only had two cops that wanted to collar up. That was my partner and me. The other officers in the squad just wanted to answer calls only unless it was a must-arrest situation. They really didn't like to take themselves out of service or leave their assigned sectors to help us out.

"That's when we decided to partner up with the other squad's heavy hitters. The command I worked in had about twenty cops that liked to collar. Before the shift would begin, we would go over who was looking for a collar. Then we would figure out a tactical plan to do our private operations. When I told two of the craziest motherfuckers, I knew on the job that I was going after the Obsession crew. A cop named B-dog and

Rhino they said, "You're nuts brother. We have been trying to catch that them for months.'"

"I have the perfect CI to send in to make a few buys for us tonight."

Rhino asked, "Are you using our boy, Stevie, Bat?"

"You got that right, bro. I just gave him thirty bucks to make a few buys throughout the night. I want him to go in a few times at different hours to get a good look. That way we can pounce on these fuckers and grab some of them. You alright with me using Stevie, Rhino?"

"Sure, thing Bat, I don't have him doing anything for me tonight." Rhino and I used Stevie as an informant. He was my registered CI, but Rhino had been his first handler off the books.

I sent Stevie into the Wagner houses to sniff around to find out what buildings the Obsession crew were dealing in. Within a half hour, he came back to my cruiser stinking of freshly smoked crack. I could smell the retched odor that was still clinging to his mouth. I held my breath and turned my head as he relayed the information from the first buy. "Okay my man, I want you to go back into the spot in two hours. Don't fucking disappear on me Stevie. Stay in the neighborhood. Do not head back home to the Douglas houses. It is too far of a walk to get back over here. I can't be driving you around in the cruiser with us. Ka'peash?"

"Yeah, yeah Batman, I know."

"Hey, Stevie, I am your handler and need to know your safe, this is not a fucking game. I'm responsible for keeping you alive. Your safety comes first. You understand that my man? Just do as I say, and you will make a steady cash flow with me."

"Right on my man."

"Okay, go get something to eat. Try a few slices of Pasty's pizza on First Avenue between 118th and 119th Street. It is the best pizza in Manhattan."

"Do they serve any wings there?"

"They might, but I have never eaten anything but their Italian food and pizza. Just have few slices Stevie, you will love it."

A few hours passed, and I sent him back inside the building to buy more vials. After twenty minutes, Stevie strolled back to my cruiser. "How does it look in there? How many mutts are in the lobby and in the stairwells bud?"

"There are four of them. The one wearing a blue hoodie and black jeans is the shot caller. He has one dealer. He is wearing all red and two lookouts at the entrance and rear doors. The shot caller has a piece tucked under his hoodie."

"Did you see the gun, Stevie?"

"Yeah, it is a revolver. I saw it when he waved over to the lookout watching the exit door. They are keeping their stash in a mailbox. I walked in when the shot caller was re-upping the dealer."

"Which mailbox is the shit being kept in, bud?"

"It's in the bottom left row that is closest to the stairwell door. I think it is 5E or 5F."

"You, definitely saw a gun?"

"Yes, I saw the handle of a revolver."

"Good stuff bro, I appreciate you coming down here and doing this for me. Here is another ten dollars. Take a bus or the A train back up to your place. Stay out of sight for the rest of the night."

"Cool Batman, thanks."

"I called over to B-dog and Rhino and met them on Pleasant Avenue. Funny thing Mac, those few blocks on Pleasant Ave, are a stronghold for the Italians. One of the five families have their headquarters there. The 116th Street boys. Tony Salerno from the Genovese family is the capo over there. The other older Italians refused to leave the area. They feel they were there first and have their family roots on that street. The gangs and thugs do not dare to even step foot near there. It is off limits zone to them. Even the hood rats respect the old time Italians and 116th Street crew.

"We waited for the radio to calm down where central was

not holding any calls for housing. Hondo and B-dog took the rear exit hiding in the bushes. Rhino and I bum-rushed the entrance door. I went for the shot caller and leg swept him off his feet him. Before he could react, I jammed my knee against his head and cuffed him up. I recovered a loaded 38 snub nose revolver. Rhino did his signature move and pile drove the dealer into the ground like he was fucking rag doll. The two lookouts bolted for the rear exit into the waiting arms of B-dog and Hondo. The mailbox that Stevie said the drugs were being kept was partially locked. The top left corner was pulled out. I grabbed my knife and pried it open. Inside there was seven bundles of pink tops and several stacks of cash, which were wrapped with rubber bands. The total taken off the street that night was seven hundred forty vials of crack, a loaded 38 revolver and three thousand dollars in cash. We collared all four players in the game that night.

"When I had gotten them back to the station house, Rhino and I took a crack at them. I wanted to see if one of them would flip on the Obsession crew. The only one that offered any information was the dealer. I knew it would be him or the shot caller. That's because they were the two who were facing the major charges. All I had been able to get out of him were the names of the two main bosses. George and Bob from the Bronx.

"I was only able to collar twelve of the members in that gang when I was on patrol. Later as time went on Bob switched over to the heroin game and combined forces with one of my most formidable foes. Purple City on 122nd Street across from Wagner. That crack organization ruled Harlem. Both Purple top and the Obsession crews dominated Second and Third Avenue from 122nd to 124th Streets. The heroin was controlled by the Obsession crew and the crack was all the Purple top. Both of those gangs were so ruthless when they joined forces, no other drug outfits dared to challenge them. That is the war story for tonight, brother." Mac told me a cool story of how he and his partner foiled an armed robbery of a cash checking store. He had received a nice medal and commendation for that collar.

When he was telling me what had taken place, I had jokingly said, "Come on brother, that is a normal shift for a NYC housing cop." We both had a nice laugh.

The motto of a housing cop is, "Second to None." There are no truer words either.

CHAPTER SEVENTEEN

While Mac and I were in Cayuga, we did everything in our power to keep busy and stay out of our cell. Mac worked in the mailroom in the mornings and afternoons five days a week. I held three jobs working seven days a week. I was the porter down on Z block which was the hole–better known as solitary confinement. I worked the morning and night shifts down on that dreadful floor. Then, in the afternoon, I worked in the mailroom after Mac pulled a few strings with his supervisor and secured me the spot.

We had a daily and evening ritual. I'd made what we called the Jenna Jameson shrine above my cabinet on the wall. It had several pictures of Jenna in compromising positions which revealed her porn-star body. So, in the morning as we would pass the magazine pictures to one another and give Ms. Jameson a big salute saying, "Good morning, Jenna. Have a terrific day." Then, at night we would blow her a kiss and say at the same time, "Goodnight, Jenna, pleasant dreams."

We even had the morning shift C. O's saying good morning to the pictures as well. It was hilarious hearing these straight nosed officers stopping at our cell door shouting, "Morning, lady Jenna."

On Tuesdays and Thursdays, I went to an alcohol addiction group. Truth was I wasn't an alcoholic, but I wanted out of my cell as much as possible. So, I lied and said that I drank a lot on the job.

I loved to play the ponies and was an avid horse racing handicapper. I guess that constituted me as a gambling addict.

We would have a two-hour session in the rec room discussing our addictions. The chairs were arranged in a large circle and the sponsor would give advice to the inmates. The counselor's name was Susan Cruz. She and her husband worked in the facility. He worked as a guard in the general population part of the prison.

As the months passed, I had noticed Mrs. Cruz staring in my direction several times during the meetings in a flirtatious manner. I didn't know how to take it at that time. I kept thinking, "You fucking dope, your imagination is getting the worst of you. Maybe because you haven't been with a woman in a long time. Stop being an idiot."

During one of the sessions, she decided to sit next me. She had crossed her legs and her right foot was right next to my calf. I tried to pay it no mind. She was wearing a nice pair of brown shoes with high heels.

Then, her foot brushed along the back of my calf. At first, I told myself, "Okay that was an accidental touch, stay cool, Pete."

Then it happened a second and third time. After that, her foot found a place behind my calf and slowly began brushing it back and forth. I will be perfectly honest with you, the feeling of a woman's touch in any capacity sent an electric bolt running through me. Even if it was just a slight brushing of her foot.

After the meeting, I couldn't wait to get back to my cell and tell Mac what had transpired. I walked into the cell like a proud peacock sticking my chest out like I was Hercules. I waited for the officer to get out of listening distance. "Why do you look like you just screwed Jenna?"

"You ready for some crazy shit, brother?"

"This sounds juicy. What happened in the meeting, Pete?"

"You aren't going to believe me, Mac. Remember I told you on several occasions the counselor, Mrs. Cruz, was looking at me during the meetings?"

"Yeah, why? What did she do today?"

"Mac, she sat right next to me, and halfway through the meeting she crossed her legs. Her right foot hit the back of my leg several times. I thought it was just a just an accidental brush the first time. Then, three more times her foot hit the back of my calf. After the last time, her foot stayed behind my leg and started to brush up and down against the back of my calf."

"Pete, you're a fucking nut and imagining things. It was accidental man. Her husband is a C.O. Do you really think she would try to fuck around with an inmate in the same jail that she and her husband work at? Okay, let us just say it happened. Did you get excited by her touch?"

"Come on Mac, I get a hard when the fucking wind blows."

"You're one crazy bastard, Peter."

"Mac, you have to join the group and see for yourself. Then, tell me if I am hallucinating this shit."

The next week Mac's request to be a part of the group was approved. During Mac's first session, we sat on opposite sides, that way he could perform his little investigation of the sultry counselor. Mrs. Cruz sat on the left side of the circle. Mac introduced himself to the group and relayed how his addiction began and spun out of control. I was laughing to myself as he gassed it up making it good and juicy. Then, the other inmates spoke about their week and how they were coping with being incarcerated.

Mac began to analyze Cruz. She had her eyes on me more than a few times during group. Her stare was seductive to say the least. I was getting extremely nervous. I didn't want any problems with the C.O.'s. But in reality, I liked the attention. She was an average looking woman, not someone I would call a looker, but when you're inside, any woman starts to look good.

When Mac and I got back to the cell, I waited by the door and made sure the coast was clear. I had to be positive no guards were in the hallway before we spoke about what had occurred during the meeting.

"Holy shit, Pete, you 're dead on about her. She is really into you. Man, you've got to be extremely careful, brother. She will get you jammed up if you ever do something with her. If you get caught, you're done for. You'll be risking everything you've fought for in here."

"What the fuck do I do Mac?"

"Just keep doing the meetings then get the hell out of dodge and get paroled."

Two weeks before I was due to be released, I was called into a back room on the tier. It was Mrs. Cruz. She greeted me and told me, "Please, Pete, take a seat."

I was sitting across from her as she completed my evaluation forms. My feet were under the desk and her foot kept touching my boot. "Well, Pete, I think we both know how I feel about you."

"Mrs. Cruz, I don't want any trouble."

"Pete, I wrote you a letter. Read it later when you go to your cell and let me know what you think at the next group. That meeting will be your last one before you are released."

She handed me the folded-up letter, and I went back to my cell. I was so nervous my hands were shaking, and I was sweating up a storm. Mac was finishing up his prayers when I finally said, "Mac, she gave me a letter."

"Well read it brother."

"Oh, holy shit! She wants to meet when I'm released. Like, that day brother." The letter went on to say that she liked me and wanted to be more than friends.

The day I was released, Susan met my family and I at a diner and we ate breakfast together. We exchanged numbers and agreed to meet later sometime in November. Several weeks passed by and I drove upstate to meet her. We met every few weeks Upstate. During one of our encounters, I asked, "Susan, how long has your husband been abusing you?"

"He is not abusing me. Why do you ask such a silly question like that?"

"On two separate occasions you came into group with a broken arm, then a black eye. When we asked you what happened? You would always answer with the same response,

'I took a misstep and tripped down some stairs.' I'll ask you again, how long has he been beating you? Take your time with the answer. If I think you're lying, I'll go to the hospitals where you live. One way or the other, I'll get the medical reports on the incidents."

"Okay, he beats me when he drinks. He is an alcoholic. He has been screwing around on me for years."

"So, this is pay back, right?"

"Yes, it is. He is a real bastard to my son and I." That was the last time I drove up to meet with her.

Around the fourth month of my parole, the officer who handled my case told me to report to his office forthwith. My P.O., Mr. Taylor, was a great guy. He had tried in vain to get me onto the fire department in the city. If I would have gotten into the NYFD, my city time would have been applied. I'd only have to do ten years as a firefighter, but the city wasn't having any of that and put an axe to his request.

I raced over to the parole office and sat at Mr. Taylor's desk. He took his seat, took a deep breath, and asked me, "What the fuck are you doing, Pete? Are you screwing a woman Upstate?"

"Yes... how did you know about that?"

"Well, her husband is coming down to Brooklyn. He requested your home address. The guy wants to speak with you. He is a corrections officer and works at the same jail where you were incarcerated. His wife works there as an addiction's counselor. Are you out of your mind, bud? I want to help you in any way I can, but my hands are going to be tied here."

"What do I do officer Taylor?"

"Well, you didn't hear this from me, understand?"

"Yes sir, loud and clear."

"If that douchebag comes to your house and starts anything, drag his ass into the house and beat the living fuck out of him. Then, call the 911 operator to report a crime in progress. Say you caught him in your house burglarizing it."

"Why are you helping me on this, Officer Taylor?"

"The guy was a total dickhead to me on the phone. He kept calling you a dirty cop. I wasn't having any of that shit. So, I told him to screw off. By the way, you're to report back here in the morning. Be early, okay? Go home and stay out of trouble. Pete, put an end to this little affair with her today."

"I already did that, sir. Thank you for having my six."

That night, my home phone rang. It was her husband on the other end, "Hey, mother fucker, since you want to fuck my wife, I am going to fuck you, right in your ass and get you sent back up here. I'll have you placed in general population. If the inmates don't kill you first, then I will. I'm going to tell your children's mother what a cheating scumbag you are."

"That's okay, she already knows that. It's a mutual thing between us."

"You think I'm fucking around with you? You're coming back here, and you'll never see the light of day again. Stay away from my slut wife. You understand me?"

"Yes, I understand completely, Mr. Cruz." I hung up the phone and made a few phone calls to some cop friends who knew a few state troopers Upstate. I let them know how the officer was abusing Susan. I told them not to fill any reports out yet. Just to keep them in a safe place. If need be, I would use that information against Mr. Cruz. It would be my Trump card if he tried anything.

The next morning, I was sitting on a bench with a bunch of parolees in the waiting room.

"Thron, go to room F."

Officer Taylor was waiting for me out in the hallway. "Pete, as of now I'm no longer your parole officer. Officer Candice Jackson will be handling your case from here on out. She is a hard ass and will violate you in a second if you fuck up. Today is the last day I'll be assisting you."

"Sorry, if I jammed you up in anyway, Officer Taylor."

"No worries brother, and I do mean brother. I know you were only doing your job and trying to clean up the streets."

As I entered the room, there were four New York state correction officers sitting in chairs.

"Sit down convict. We know all about you and Mrs. Cruz. By the way she has been terminated. You, on the other hand, have violated your parole. You traveled Upstate"

"What are you talking about, I never left NY."

"No, you didn't leave New York, but you left the county you live in and never asked for permission to do so. That is a violation of parole, and you just might be coming back up with us. Officer Cruz wanted to be here today, but we advised him to stay away from you. We thought it would be in your best interest that he isn't present. He is well aware of all the things you did with his wife. What is your phone number, convict?"

"Why do you need that? It is on the jacket you have in front of you on the desk."

"Well, we are going to call your children's mother and let her know what you have been up to."

"Go right ahead, let her know."

"Stand up and put your hands behind your back."

"Before I do that, what am I being violated for?"

"You left the county without any permission."

"Okay, just so you are all aware, Officer Cruz is a spouse abuser, and he will be charged by the state police on several felony charges. That is, if I don't leave the building a free man. I've already checked Mrs. Cruz's hospital records and all the allegations will hold up."

"Sit the fuck down convict."

The officer that was questioning me got on the phone with Mr. Cruz and told him what would take place if I was violated. A few minutes later the four officers surrounded me and gave me specific instructions never to contact Susan again. I walked out of the Brooklyn building a free man.

I made sure to stay away from Mrs. Cruz. Twenty years later I reconnected with my old friend Mac. He had told me how I was caught screwing Mrs. Cruz. Mac's cellmate, Dave, was snooping around the cell and found the letter she had written me before I was released. For some reason, I had forgotten to take it with me. Dave read the letter and ratted me out to the corrections officers. Mac was visited several times in his cell and roughed up and threatened by Mr. Cruz.

The corrupt officer told Mac he was going to be put in general population. Mac never ratted me out. Even with all the threats Cruz and his cronies threw at him, he remained true to the blue wall of silence. He is what is known as a true-blue brother. They placed Mac in solitary confinement for thirty days for his loyalty to me.

CHAPTER EIGHTEEN

What is the first thing the prison system does to an inmate when they are locked up? The answer is simple, they try to break you. At first, they attempt to destroy any hope you're holding onto. Then, the corrections officers try to crush any thoughts you have left in your mind for a life after being incarcerated. What are the last words any inmate hears before the gates open when passing the final guard at the exit gate? "Don't be coming back here. I do not want to see your sorry ass come through my prison again."

The word rehabilitation is such a fucking joke when a person steps inside those four walls that are surrounded by high razor fences. There is big money for all the parties who have their hands in the prison till. The officials who run the jails are banking on the inmate to be set free and commit a crime while on the outside. That's the law of the jungle. I knew I had to be more than a number to the system. I couldn't let the system, a corrections officer or a convict break me.

The pressure I faced every day while being a prisoner was so taxing. All I had was my beliefs and my will to survive. I would always look forward to every other Sunday. One reason was because I knew my family was coming up to visit me. The other was because on those Sunday nights, a handful of thc inmates on my block would have an Italian dinner. Being that I was one of the only Italians on the tier, I volunteered to cook dinner. Only for a handful of inmates whom I had some trust in. The Thursdays before the dinner, we would go down to commissary to purchase what we needed for the next two weeks.

The group would buy Boboli pizza sauce and mozzarella

cheese. Then I collected all the sauce and cheese and a few packs of Ramen noodles or pasta. I would add the spices, salt, pepper, onion powder, garlic powder and Sazon Goya seasoning. Let me put it this way, it wasn't my mother's sauce, that's for damn sure. But it was good enough for what I had available to me while inside.

One night while I laid in my bunk, I was thinking about my academy days. When a police recruit walked through the front lobby, they had to stop and salute the officers at the front desk. I would walk into the lobby, stop, then snap my salute. It was always crisp.

One day the officer behind the desk stopped me after I had saluted him and told me, "Probationary police officer Thron, you have the best salute we have seen in several years. Keep up the good work officer."

That compliment gave me a sense of pride and still does. I also had been a sharpshooter with my pistol, which was a nice accolade. Sharp shooters and pistol experts could wear a bar on their shield holder signifying their status. But by far my best accomplishment in the academy was learning to the drive the RMP (radio patrol car).

All recruits must pass a driving test to be an operator in a cop car. The driving course is at Floyd Bennett Field in Brooklyn. We were all timed during our tests. The instructor informed us, "Whoever does the course the fastest gets to do the highway patrol course."

Well that was yours truly, and it was such a rush to do it. At one point, I had the cruiser going ninety miles per hour on the straight away of the obstacle course.

While I gazed up at the ceiling that night, I kept saying to myself, "Damn being a cop is truly one of the most fulfilling and dangerous jobs in the world."

I missed the action of making drug busts and taking guns off the street. How many men and women do you know run into a situation where they have no connection with the people that are in harm's way? Cops and other law enforcement agencies do without any hesitation. They are a rare breed.

Then I heard a loud noise in the hallway–it sounded like gunfire. One of the C.O.'s had punched a locker in the control room. Our cell was the closet to the officer's office so we could hear a lot of things they spoke about when the door was left open. After I heard the loud bang, I sprang up quickly into a sitting position which had shook the bunk.

"What the fuck Pete, are you okay brother?"

"Yeah, I am good, Mac. The noise just put me back on the street for a second. Sorry if I broke your concentration while you were reading."

I slowly lowered my head back onto my pillow. The thoughts of gunfire raced through my head. I closed my eyes and seized the moment. I entered my old world and let my mind and soul drift into my past life. I pictured myself back in Harlem. I could hear the bad guys firing their weapons. They were either committing violent crimes against innocent people or retaliating against a rival drug gang. But then there were the blockheads who just would shoot their guns in the air for no apparent reason. It always amazed me how those jack asses never thought the bullets would come crashing back down. The perps paid no mind to the fact or the possibility a projectile could kill an innocent bystander.

I said to Mac, "Hey do you realize how crazy cops are? We're the only people who aren't in the military that run into a gun fight. The normal citizen hauls ass from gunfire. Not us, we run right smack dab into a fire fight. How fucking insane is that?"

"Yeah, Pete, we definitely have problems in the thinking department upstairs. It's why we're inside."

"Well, I'll tell you two things, brother. I can handle the mental problems upstairs. I just never want any problems downstairs with the other head. Man, if someone had to walked into our cell at this moment and tell me, 'You can have your job back.' I would give my right nut, to be dodging bullets for the next fucking twenty years. I wouldn't hesitate with that decision. I miss being a cop, Mac."

"I know you do, Pete. Try to get some sleep man. We're stuck in here and need to stay strong. Let's keep our minds focused on getting out and back into the real world."

"Amen to that, brother."

Summertime at Cayuga was brutal due to the insects crawling and flying around. I was getting close to my parole hearing in late August of 1998, and it was scorching hot during the nighttime during that month. The rec room windows were surrounded by flood lights which were attached to the outside of the building. There were thousands of mosquitoes buzzing around the lights that night.

Two jerkoff inmates decided to play games and opened all the windows of the room. The insects swarmed inside and attacked us. It was complete chaos. The guards grabbed us and had us facing our cell doors.

They had quickly closed the rec room door, then gave us orders, "On the count of three enter your cells. If you need medical attention kneel on the floor and keep your right hand raised in the air. We are sending for the medical staff now."

I had been bitten hundreds of times. My body was covered in bites. The insects had sent little doses of venom into me. I was sick for three days with a high fever and was constantly throwing up. It felt like I had the flu. The bites were so irritating, all I wanted to do was tear my skin from my body. The other inmates suffered the same bodily disorders. None of the inmates reported to work for three days.

The C.O.'s was extremely pissed off at the two morons who had pulled that stunt. It is safe to say they both received beatings by the hands of the guards and several infuriated convicts.

Many times, while being incarcerated in Cayuga, the sweltering heat would drain my body. My body would be soaked in sweat. The only way to get relief was to lay next to the cell door. At the bottom of the door was an inch and half gap so I'd lay down and press my face against the cool floor and let the hallway breeze hit me.

During the winter months it was the complete opposite. We froze our asses off. Mac and I slept in our bunks fully clothed. Sometimes, we would even wear our prison issued jackets for the extra warmth. The good thing was the bottom half of the window opened three inches and it was encased in a metal cage. So, we never had to worry about keeping any food fresh that needed to be kept refrigerated. We placed our drinks and food products on the windowsill to keep them frozen. It worked out well most of the time.

Mac and I were blessed to have families that kept us well stocked with food and cigarettes. Our families would speak on the phone and coordinate who would bring certain food and other supplies we needed for the month. I am so grateful to my family for being there for me during that hellish time in my life.

CHAPTER NINETEEN

To this day I will never be able to understand, or accept, a man or woman committing a sexual crime against another person. I am a true believer that any person that perpetrates a sexual act against a child must never see the light of day and that any person who rapes a woman should be castrated and or sentenced to life in prison. I will never be able to comprehend such deviant thoughts or acts. I often think to myself, if that person is so desperate to get a woman to have sex with them consensually, then go out and pay someone who is willing. Why prey on the innocent women who never did them any harm? If I was in the special victim's unit while a cop, I would have administered my own brand of justice and the offenders would have never made it to trial. If that constitutes me as a dirty cop, then so be it.

As I've mentioned, Cayuga was designated as a sexual predator facility. I would say fifty percent of the inmates in that penitentiary housed those scum bags. That was, and is still, a hard pill for me to swallow.

On the tier I was on, ten to twelve inmates were sexual offenders. Mac and I stayed clear of them at all times. It didn't matter if they were trying to be polite to us, I wanted nothing to do with them. Most of the other inmates stayed clear as well. I know the Latinos would have slit their throats had the opportunity presented itself.

Two convicts that really infuriated me went by the names Billy and Tom. Billy was this hick from Upstate, he had, long red hair and liked to watch pro wrestling. He would train in the yard and from watching him lift, I could tell he was strong. When he first arrived in Cayuga the corrections officers didn't give any of us the heads up about him being a sexual offender. Tom's first week, he had formed several friendships with a few inmates. Mac and I had a bad feeling about the guy from the start. There was something behind the prick's eyes that just housed something evil.

One night in the yard, I had finished my training early and joined some of the inmates to walk the yard. We had done a few laps when Frank/Fran said, "What the fuck is going on over there? Is the red headed freak humping into the guy he is spotting while he's doing squats?"

We all turned and saw the guy imitating a humping motion while working out with his partner. He wasn't touching him, but it was apparent what he was thinking.

The yard officer yelled out, "Wrap it up convicts, yard time is over in five minutes."

When we went into the rec room that night, we called the guy over who was training with Bill.

I said to Steve, "Hey dude, we need to give you a heads up about your training partner, Red."

"What's up, what's going on?"

"Okay while we were walking, and you were squatting, your boy was emulating humping your ass."

"Are you shitting me bro?"

"No, my friend, we figured we would give you a heads up so you can be prepared for a proposal."

After I had made that remark the entire table broke out into a frenzy of an uncontrollable laughter.

"We need to find out what this guy's story is. I'll ask Robinson tomorrow when I see him down on Z-block. For the time being, don't train with that freak. Well, that is unless you're thinking about hooking up with him."

"You guys are such assholes." Again, we broke out in laughter.

The next night I inquired about what the guy Bill had been

convicted for. "Okay Officer Robinson, what did he do?"

"You sure you want to hear this, Pete?"

"Don't tell me he is a sexual predator."

"He is the worst kind brother. He raped a little girl and sodomized a seven-year-old boy. Pete, he is an extremely dangerous violent convict. He has already been in for ten years at maximum facilities. The last year and half, he was rewarded for good behavior. They lessened his security clearance and now he is eligible for all medium facilities. Don't let your guard down on this guy. He's violent and has raped a few inmates and stabbed several others. He's never getting out. He's a lifer now with all the extra charges he caught while doing his original bid."

"Thank you, Officer Robinson, for the information. You okay with me telling a few of the guys upstairs?"

"Sure thing, but you didn't hear any of this from me."

"Of course not, I have your six, Robinson."

The following night when we were doing our usual walk around the yard, a few of the inmates wanted to know what the deal was with Bill.

An inmate Cortez asked, "What's this mother fucker's deal, Bro?"

"Listen guys, this isn't good at all. First things first. This isn't coming from me or my guy on Z-block. Is everyone cool with that? If not, then just break off from the walk, okay?"

"Pete, we need to know. Some of us still have our allegiances to our other brothers in general pop. The shot callers of the Neta's and Kings will send us our orders."

"That's fine guys but remember it's not coming from me or the C.O. downstairs."

"No problem Pete, you have our word on that."

"Remember snitches get stitches. I'm too fucking close to my parole hearing, but this shit head needs to be dealt with by us or an outsider faction. The word is, he is a pedophile, and it's come from a reliable source."

A king named Acosta asked, "What did this scumbag do?

I need as much information, so I can get it out to my people in general pop."

"He raped a little girl and sodomized a seven-year-old boy."

The King spoke in Spanish to the other Latino inmates that were walking with us.

"Brothers let the Kings deal with this piece of shit. I'm asking you all to give it to us." The Neta's all agreed to hand Bill over to the Kings.

The guard called, "Let's get going convicts, yard time is finished."

That night in the rec room I could see all the Spanish inmates were waiting for Bill to make one mistake. They were just biding their time and waiting on orders for the green light–they'd do Bill on the spot.

I was able to rest my head on my pillow that night without feeling a morsel of guilt about for relaying the information on the pedophile.

The Spanish guys on the tier wanted to be the soldiers to administer the beating on Bill, but he knew that the entire floor was onto him and the charges he had been guilty of. The child rapist begged the C.O.'s to have him transferred or be thrown into solitary confinement. The next week, he was sent off to another facility before the hit could be carried out. I said good riddance to that low-life bastard.

When cops enter the prison system, they are categorized by the correction officers and the inmates. Depending on that individual's offenses and what they have been convicted of determines how they'll be dealt with. That rule is pretty much set-in stone for all convicts. But cops are dealt with entirely different and the level of psychological and physical warfare that is brought down upon them can be extremely violent. Therefore, they are sent into protective custody, but, unfortunately, P.C. is not a safe place to be anymore. If they want you dead or beaten to a pulp, they'll get to you.

About six months in Cayuga, a new arrival came onto the floor. Robinson and the other officers had already alerted all of us of the man's offenses. He was a vile disgusting pedophile who was caught with thousands of underground videos and pictures of children.

The evidence found on his computer was one of the worst cases the Special Victim's Unit in Orange County had ever come across. There were hours and hours of videos of children being exploited and forced to have sex with each other and adults. As I write this part of the story, my stomach is in knots, but I felt it needed to be written about and relayed to you readers. These types of criminals created some of the horrors of my prison life. The reason for that is I can't get the vile acts they perpetrated on those little angels out of my head. The offenders' victims need justice and closure. I hope to give them that, by writing the truth and exposing their attackers.

The new inmate was a monster. Worst of all, he was also a cop. Someone who was supposed to protect little children from demons like himself. He exploited innocent minors for his own pleasure and monetary gains. He would sell pictures and videos that he obtained through a secret group he belonged to.

Tom had become a cop in the late eighties in Upstate Orange County. He was a clean-cut man that looked like a throwback from the seventies. He kind of looked like a textbook nerd. Just seeing that prick's face in the morning and during rec would fill me with rage.

Tom walked around the place like he owned it. He didn't have a care in the world. The worst part was that he often proclaimed his innocence in the addiction group.

One day in group, he was trying to explain to us that the evidence against him was false. He swore that it wasn't his computer the smut was found on.

"I swear guys, it was another colleague's computer. Pete, Mac, you guys believe me, right? You know how it is. The Blue Wall of Silence. I am a Blue Brother, right?"

Mac turned to me and said, "I will let you handle this one, bro."

I looked around the circle and got the nod from the other inmates. I was one of them while I was inside those prison walls, but I needed to be a cop for five minutes during the group.

AD said, "Do your thing, Pete and be that cop you once were."

The counselor was fidgeting and nervous. I looked at the daytime C.O. He just nodded for me to proceed. He knew I wasn't going to jeopardize my freedom for a pedophile.

I stood up from my chair and walked over to Tom. "Let me tell you something, cocksucker. Don't ever call Mac and I your brother. You aren't a brother in blue. You're the worst scum on this earth. I wish my brothers behind me could tear you to shreds, but they'll let this play out and watch it all unfold. That's because your hell is just beginning in here. It'll only get worse when you get out. You'll have to register yourself as a sex offender for the rest of your life. Anywhere you live, the neighborhood and schools your children attend, will know your dirty little secret. I hope your children later in their lives understand the severity of your sickness and disgusting ways. Hopefully, they'll never accept you back into their lives."

Tom just stayed silent, and tears rolled down his cheeks. Then Bull shouted to him, "I will slap the white off your face if you shed another tear."

Tom asked to be excused from the meeting and went back to his cell. He didn't leave his cell for three days until he felt things had calmed down.

The last week of my incarceration, my sister and cousin had taken the trip up to visit me. Tom was sitting at a table in a row across from us. His wife and two small children were there. His son and younger daughter. That's correct, I said his two young children.

During the visit, two events took place. The first being my sister told that she felt the eyes of one of the general population inmates staring at her in an inappropriate way. I told her and my cousin to only look at me while they were in the visiting room. I was holding a plastic fork in my right hand from the lunch they'd purchased for me from the vending machine. I had formed the four prongs of the folk into a triangular shape. Just in case I needed to shove it into the inmate's eye. Yes, I may have been going home in a week, but my sense of loyalty to my family still came first and always will. I needed to protect my family by any means necessary. Luckily, the rest of the visit went smooth, and nothing occurred.

The second thing that happened was when the ex-cop pedophile was bouncing his little girl on his lap. The bastard seemed to be enjoying it a little too much. For a few minutes, I observed Tom who was occasionally gyrating against his daughter backside. Tom had a big old smile on his face during the visit. While he was bouncing his daughter up and down on his lap he was making out with his wife.

I wanted to snap that fucker's neck and end him right there. The visit ended, and I said my goodbyes to my sister and cousin. I knew I would be going home in less than a week. I just needed to stay focused a little while longer.

A few days later, I advised the addiction counselor of what I had witnessed Tom doing during his visit. She assured me that she would alert the chain of command and have Tom dealt with later. To me this wasn't snitching on any of those sick men. It was all about doing the right thing and keeping those perverted monsters away from other innocent children and women.

CHAPTER TWENTY

During my extended vacation, which is what I like to call my two-year bid, I came across how some of the inmates coped with their incarceration. One of the ways was to get high on illegal drugs, which they would have a family member stuff inside one of their cavities.

Make no mistake, narcotics run deep inside the prison walls. Many of the inmates were addicted to drugs while out on the street. Some had to go cold turkey when they were first incarcerated and then try as hard as they could to stay straight, but many of them needed their fix so they can handle being locked up. The need to get high becomes too great for some of them.

There many reasons convicts fall off the wagon or begin to use narcotics inside prison. Some are assaulted by other violent offenders who prey on the weaker ones. Some are brutally sodomized, either in the mouth or ass.

If an intimate who had addiction problems fell victim to one of these dreadful acts there are only three ways out. Either fight back and risk grave injury or death, submit to the beatings and the sexual assaults bestowed upon them, or turn back to getting high on drugs or become first time users. If they chose the latter option, the addicted inmate would often ask a friend or family member to smuggle some heroin or cocaine into the facility.

What I couldn't comprehend was how a person could look into their mother's or sister's eyes and ask them to insert a dangerous narcotic up their vagina or anus. It seems too selfish and heinous an act. To have them risk going to prison for smuggling contraband into a prison facility is just an atrocious request. The person smuggling the drugs into the penitentiary also risks possible fatal intoxication if one of the packets breaks open. And depending on the length of time the narcotics were released inside their body; it could pose a fatality.

When I spoke with a convict named Dave, who was heavily addicted to heroin, I asked him, "Davey aren't you nervous your mother will get caught and be sent to prison?"

His response just floored me.

"Listen, I know you're an ex-copper, but I have to do what's needed to survive in here. I hate being locked up in this freaking place. So, that's the only way I can escape this shit hole for a few hours. When I get to ride that magic carpet and forget where I really am, I feel like I'm not here anymore for that short time."

"Davey, that's your mother we're speaking about. What the fuck man?"

"She's willing to take the chance for me."

"So, you think that makes it right? It is so wrong and unethical to ask and have your mother do. I don't know how you can live with yourself knowing what you're asking her to risk. Just so you can get your next fix."

"It is what it is, Pete."

At that moment I felt like choking the life out of that piece of crap.

Then there was another indulgence many inmates partook in. Drinking the prison hooch. The bootlegger on the block was a guy named Tito. He was one big bastard and knew how to throw his hands in a fight. But he was a gentle giant on the inside.

On the streets in the Bronx, he was gang banger. Inside, no inmate wanted any part of him when it came to going head-to-head in an altercation. They knew if someone tangled with Tito, they would get fucked up beyond all recognition. Plus, the inmate would get blacklisted from being served Tito's special hooch.

One night we were playing cards when some of the other inmates begged him for taste of the good stuff. Inmate Cruz asked, "Tito can we get a few shots tonight? Is the new batch ready yet?"

"Let me check to see if she's ready fellas. Pete, you want to take a walk and stand guard for me. Just so no officers see me grabbing the hooch?"

"Sure, I'll stand in front of your cell door, brother."

As we made our way to his cell he said, "This will only take a second. I need to smell it and taste the goods first. I have to make sure the booze is ready. I don't want anyone to get alcohol poisoning."

"You are shitting me, right?"

"No man, my batches are extremely potent and will get you drunk on one or two shots at most."

He did his taste test then shook the cobwebs from his head. "Oh, yeah brother she's ready. Just like a nice virgin."

We walked back into the rec room and resumed playing. I took a shot of Tito's prison moonshine and it fucking floored me.

"Holy shit that is the strongest alcohol I've ever tasted."

The game ended within twenty minutes. No one was up for playing anymore. We all had a nice buzz going and wanted to enjoy it.

"Tito, what is your secret to success with this crazy hooch?"

He went on to explain the process, breaking it down in steps for me.

"Okay brother, this is what I do. There are several ways to make it. You have different types of wine. Potato wine, tomato wine, and the one we just drank which is my favorite, fruit wine. The ingredients are amazingly simple. You need water, and sugar. The problem I run into often is the amount of sugar needed to make the wine. If I make the potato or tomato wine, I use two pounds of sugar to every gallon of water I make.

Fruit wine only needs one pound for each gallon of water. That is because the fruits are already naturally loaded with their own sugars. I use all types of fruit, oranges, pears, apples, and the big purple plums."

"Oh, the plums that look like they were ripped from a gorillas nut sack?"

"Yeah, those are the best fruit to use. Next, I either need to cook it or store it in my cell. I cut the legs off prison issued pants. I go as high as possible when I cut the legs. That usually provides me with enough room to line them with two heavy trash bags. I sew the shit out of the seams and the bottom ends–that's so the legs won't leak out any of the hooch. I then pour two and a half gallons of water into each pant leg. Then, I add about five pounds of sugar. Which is a pain in the ass to acquire in here. Five cups of diced up tomatoes and a can of tomato paste. The paste makes the hooch turn faster. Acting as real kicker.

"The moonshine starts to cook when the tomatoes rot then ferment. Which, in turn, causes the sugar to turn into alcohol. Ventilation is extremely important. I'll then roll the tops of the bags together around a pencil or pen case. I leave an opening at the top end as close as possible to let the hooch breathe. I rubber band each pants leg as tight as it can go and roll them up above the opening close to the liquid. Next, I find a good place to hang the pant legs–the warmer the better. It makes the wine cook faster. I usually put it behind my toilet. Then it's ready in twelve days. But if I use a kicker like tomato paste, potatoes or some yeast, which is extremely hard to get in here, it cuts the fermenting process down to six to nine days. If I get my hands on a small vitamin bottle, I'll add water and sugar and some old fruit or orange peels and let it rot.

"I can sell a bottle of my hooch for two cartons of smokes. If the inmate doesn't smoke and has some type of food, I'll trade for that instead of the smokes. The most dangerous part of being a moonshiner in prison is obviously getting caught by the corrections officers. I don't need to catch a new charge. It's way too close to my parole hearing to fuck up now. But I always make sure the hooch doesn't stink up my cell when I am cooking a new batch. I try to walk a straight and narrow path in here. I keep to myself and try not to cause any trouble with the guards or other inmates. The less attention I draw to myself, the better. You know what I mean, brother?"

"I completely get what you're saying, Tito. I'll tell you this. That is the strongest shit I've ever tasted."

"Thank you, Pete, for the compliment. Keep your head down and get home to your family."

CHAPTER TWENTY-ONE

There were so many pieces to the puzzle while I was incarcerated. I had no other choice but to figure out a way to put them together, and I had to do it quickly. First, I had to deal with the other inmates and learn to adapt to my surroundings. Closing the door to my heart and soul and forgetting I was a cop was one of the hardest things I had to force upon myself. I couldn't shut the door completely, but I closed it in a way that left enough light for me to make it back when the time came.

The second choice I made was opening myself up to my convict life. I saw firsthand that if a convict wants something from a weaker inmate, they don't ask for it, they took it from them. It could be anything from ice cubes, phone time, sneakers, smokes, food to the extreme of an inmate's body. If they wanted it, they were going to get it anyway they had to.

While being incarcerated, the only way I kept sane and survived was by keeping myself occupied. Prison is about routine. Work and training were my routines along with reading and my afternoon prayers. I was fortunate enough to have a person who was also from the same world I once came from, my good friend and brother, Mac.

When my sentence was coming to an end, I experienced how medieval the prison facility's medical and dental practices were.

I was experiencing a lot of pain in my front teeth, so I made an appointment with the dentist. However, it took several weeks to get approved–maybe I should call him the Horror Dentist.

I needed two root canals on my front choppers. The doctor said, "I am going to give you a few Novocain shots to numb the front of your mouth."

I was trying to be polite to the guy and said, "Sounds good, Doc. How bad is this going to feel?"

"Stop being a baby. You'll be fine. I am going to do the whole procedure today. It usually requires two visits, but we will complete the entire procedure today."

I hate dentists to begin with. Not to offend any of my dental readers. I had several bad encounters with them in the past. I wasn't thrilled to say the least about what I was going to be experiencing for the next hour and half.

The doctor went to work with his drill and his sadistic tools. Towards the end, when he was placing that screw instrument in my teeth to secure the post, he had an evil smile on his face.

"Please rinse out your mouth."

I swished the water around, then spit it out. I saw a ton of blood as my backwash drained down the sink.

"Fuck, why am I bleeding so much, Doc?"

"You'll be fine. Put your head back down and relax. You're almost finished."

I looked at a metal instrument he was holding, he began heating the tip of it. A few seconds later he shoved the tool up to the roof of my mouth into the spot where he had performed the root canal. A burning pain shot up into my head and the scent of the burning flesh in the roof of my mouth filled the room. My teeth were on fire and my brain felt like it had been pierced with a hot fireplace poker. My front teeth seared when my tongue touched them.

"Rinse out again, you're all done. Guard he is ready to be escorted back to his cell." The Horror Dentist just shot me that sadistic smile of his.

I went back into the cell and Mac greeted me. "How are

you feeling, brother? What the hell is that smell. It smells like something is burning."

"Take a look inside my mouth, brother."

"What in fucks name did he do to you?"

"He cauterized the two teeth he did the root canals on. I was bleeding a lot, so he heated something up and stuck it up into my teeth and the roof of my mouth. That bastard seemed to be enjoying the pain he was inflicting on me. Don't get any dental work done in this shit hole."

When it came to any medical treatment, an inmate must request to see the nurse or doctor. There are times a request is deemed a non-emergency and may be delayed or denied. It's my opinion that there are too few doctors and nurses to provide the proper medical treatment for inmates. Referrals and medication refills for some reason too often fall through the cracks. An inmate who has been injured or sick can be ordered to return to their cell before they are healed from their injury or sickness.

Prisoners that have existing health issues may not get the proper care or medication that is required to keep them healthy. At times, when these needs are not met by the prison staff, those health problems will without a doubt worsen. I know firsthand that Cayuga officials tried to keep the facility as clean as possible. But the truth of the matter is, it was unhealthy and unhygienic. There's poor control of many infectious diseases in the correctional system. The health issues are a serious problem in the facilities throughout New York State.

When it comes to the inmates who have mental health issues, that is an entirely different animal to tame. Those individuals are a danger to themselves and to the other inmates around them. They can go off at the drop of a dime. Then, anyone around them is at grave risk. Inmates like that shouldn't be incarcerated and should rather be in a mental health facility, where they can be monitored twenty-four hours a day. If the correctional system responded to the mental health problems in the correct way, the quality of life of a vast number of inmates would improve tremendously.

If a career criminal gets incarcerated, it is like he is going back to school. It is a place where they'll have a bed and three-square meals provided for them. Jail is where the convict has time to hone his craft a strengthen his skills. They'll reach out to other inmates that have been collared for the same crimes and swap information and knowledge. These convicts are extremely dangerous to society.

I've said it before, and I'll say it again. Murderers, rapist, three-time losers, and child molesters should never see the light of day again. Those violent felons deserve to rot in hell. It is unfortunate that the bail reform came into existence. It's used to reduce the use of our jails and increase fairness of the justice system. But the lawmakers and politicians have let many violent felons out on early release. It also allows the offender the right to know an informant or witnesses name. They get to face their accusers before the trial starts. No good will ever come out of that.

The offender is granted full disclosure of their victim's or victims' personal information. This in turn has led to several victims being murdered. The New York legislators have tied all law enforcements' hands. The judges must follow the new guidelines and can't impose proper punishment against the violent criminals that stand before them. The mayor and governor have handed the keys to the streets of New York over to the lawbreakers. The police can no longer perform their duties, due to the fear of being disciplined or losing their job and being arrested.

Being locked up taught me many lessons in life. But it is a part of my life that I cannot permit my future wife or loved ones ever to observe. My soul has many doors that I keep locked up. Some of those horrors are from when I was a cop, and others are from when I was an inmate. Those memories need to be kept locked away forever.

I was lucky enough to exit the gates of hell and be reunited with my family in one piece. The true test would be in the coming months and years. The correctional system did nothing to prepare me for the shit-show society was going to throw at me.

CHAPTER TWENTY-TWO

In 1998, I knew I was innocent of most of the charges I had been convicted of. If I was guilty of one thing it was making an entry in my memo book that was not completely true. Looking back on my time on the force, I have come to the realization that I was more than likely punished for bending the rules.

Yes, I did a lot of hot pursuit collars. I used necessary force when I needed to make a collar–maybe too much at times. Any person who hasn't put on a blue uniform or gone undercover in high pressured buy and bust, cannot understand how chaotic it gets. Within a few seconds any situation can turn into a life-threatening one. I am living proof of that.

The night in question maybe I didn't follow every procedure. But it was to protect my partners from being killed. I did as I always had done–went to gather intelligence on the higher chain of command in that drug organization or any others.

All that ever mattered to me was bringing down as many drug dealers and violent criminals as I could. So, I say, fuck the brass, the rat squad, and the criminal system who felt I needed to be made a scape goat.

Many years later, I would write my first book "End of Tour" and would be reunited with the cops who did stand by me. I was welcomed back into my blue family by all police departments throughout our great country.

I did my time in jail and I was on my way home to my children. My family was taking me away from that hell hole I had spent close to two years in.

Before going to prison, I never understood why prisoners

and ex-cons would say that the air smelled different. How they would look up into the sky and close their eyes taking the sweet smell of the fresh air for extended periods of time. But now, I know exactly what that feeling is like.

As I walked to the exit gates, I looked up at the guard tower, and snapped a salute to Officer Thompson in a respectful way. He was armed with a shotgun and shouted, "You keep your head up, Pete and good luck to you."

I nodded a yes, and he waved for the three-tier barbed wire fence that surrounded the prison ground to be opened. As it slid open slowly–this is their last way of them torturing me.

I stood outside the car door, looked at my mother, brother, and sister, and closed my eyes for a second to take it all in.

I was finally free.

"Pete, Pete," it was my brother and sister. "Pete, you ready to go home?"

Home. I was really going home. After I breathed in the air and felt the sun on my face I said, "Just one more minute guys, this all feels so surreal for me."

My mother was crying, and my brother's and sister's eyes welled with tears. As did mine. I hugged them and went to my mother and said, "I made it mom. No, we all made it out alive. Everything will be okay from now on."

Shit was I wrong.

Then they said, "Let's get you some real food."

I asked them if it would be okay if we had breakfast with the woman counselor.

"Sure, the more the merry," my sister said.

Mom blurted out, "Can we get the hell away from this place now? It always gives me the creeps coming in here."

We met up with Susan and ate breakfast for a good two hours just catching up on everyday life.

My brother pulled me to the side and asked me, "Pete, do you want to go to a hotel room for a few hours with your lady friend. It's not a problem. I'll pay for it. I'm sure you have a lot of pent-up aggression you need to release."

"No man, I'm okay. I don't want to take the chance of being caught or getting her into any kind of trouble."

Well, as you know, that would later backfire on Susan and me.

We drove for what seemed like an eternity back to my children. My heart and my soul, the reason I stayed strong were waiting for me in Brooklyn. What a surreal feeling that was.

There is no way to really put into words how I felt during that drive. All I could think about was getting home and holding my children. It was time to start my life over. My new life. A quite different one and little did I know that 24 years later I'd still be searching for that new life.

You see, I wasn't prepared for the aftermath and the dark shadow that would follow me and haunt me all day, every day. The darkness I live in is like a demon. I know we all have them. Some of us learn how to fight them, others learn to push them away. Then, there are some of us that no matter what we do they cannot and will not leave. That was me, and I didn't know it then, but my torment would be and still is the judicial system. The same one I sacrificed myself for, ended up being my affliction.

My first month home was an adjustment, I was able to get up when I wanted to, go to the bathroom, and eat whenever I wanted to. There weren't any inmates fighting over who got more ice cubes in their drinks. No fighting over phone time. Sounds simple but it took time to get used to freedom again. My children and my family were my salvation and slowly I began to adjust.

However, I slept, and still do, like shit. Never more than 1-2 hours at a time and it took years to learn that I could sleep with my eyes fully closed. After a month of showering my kids with as much love as I could, it was time to get back to work and get a job.

I had been smart enough to stash some money into my OTB, off track betting account, before I was sent away. I was a decent horse racing handicapper and hit a nice trifecta before I left on my extended vacation.

One morning I woke up and went to the attic to get a game for my kids to play and saw my uniform. The goddam fucking uniform had seen drugs busts, pedophiles, gangs, gun fights and more. It was the same one I played baseball in with the kids in Harlem. I remembered being in that uniform while I held a crying woman whose child had just been murdered. Damn my blue magnet had seen so much needless death. I would never wear that uniform again.

I stood there staring at it, tears filling my face, tears of sadness, confusion, desperation, and sheer utter grief. And then it hit me like a tidal wave. Anger and more anger, like I had never experienced before. The police brass, the judges had gotten the better of me and I couldn't do anything about it.

As the months went by, I started to get into the groove of being a father again. My family did everything in their power to help me adjust. We had very traditional Italian dinners on the holidays.

However, during this time I also started to suffer from all the injuries I had sustained while I was a cop. I now need to use a nasal spray three to four times a day to help me breath from being pistol whipped in the face. My back and neck have seven bulging and herniated discs in them. I never realized the toll the job took on me until my health started to deteriorate. That's when the nightmares worsened.

Some nights I would wake up in a sweat, screaming at some scumbag to drop his gun, or wake up holding my face thinking I had been pistol whipped again or shot.

Same alley, same job. A man with a gun who had just robbed and beaten an elderly woman. That dream keeps reoccurring to this day. Bam, bam, I get shot five or six times and my bullets hit the perp point blank, but the fucker never goes down. My rounds don't penetrate the bastard.

Then, on most nights I just dream of Judge Allen and Andrews. They'd be standing over me, larger than life, sipping a glass of water and looking down at me, smiling and laughing. In another dream, I'd see them from my jail cell motioning for me to come out, but before I could they'd slam the door shut.

Even just the sound of those cell door's shutting causes me psychological suffering and unexplainable physical pain. I wouldn't wish that upon anyone–well, maybe those two judges.

CHAPTER TWENTY-THREE

Finding work is one thing, getting an employer to overlook the felony on my record is another. The prison system sets up an inmate for the most part and advocates that they stay out of trouble. The correctional system told me to get out and be a productive member of society, what they didn't prepare me for, however, was the word "no".

I had been home for several months and was still jobless. I decided to take a chance in the industry I was an expert in–security and investigations. I drew up a resume that I felt confident would get me a position in most security companies or investigation firms.

I first applied for a security position at a high-end department store called Fortunoff's. It was supposed to pay fourteen dollars per hour.

I was called into the head of security's office. As he reviewed my resume, he looked up at me and said, "Pete, why the hell do you want to work here? You're more qualified for my position. Your training and expertise are outstanding. Why do you want to be a guard in a department store?"

"Well to be honest sir, I have been out of work for a year and half now and I need to get employment as soon as possible."

"Well as far as I'm concerned you've got the job. When can you start, Pete?"

"Right away, sir."

"Very good. I'll be in touch with you by the days end to give you your schedule."

We shook hands, and as I was walking out the door when

he said, "I just have to have my people do a background check on you. Then, you'll be good to go."

"Thank you very much, sir."

As I was driving home to Brooklyn my cell phone rang. I looked at the clock on my car radio and had been driving for about thirty-five minutes.

"Hello, this is Pete speaking. Who do I have the pleasure of speaking with?" I knew damn well who it was.

"Hey, Pete, it's Jim from Fortunoff's. Listen, turns out we can't use you because of your criminal record. Sorry, it is out of my hands, Pete."

"I understand and thank you for taking the time to interview me. Have a good day."

I slammed my fist onto the dash several time and screamed, "When is my punishment going to be over God? Haven't I suffered enough of this bullshit. Give me a break already."

Later that day, I pulled into the off-track betting parking lot. I met my good friend Louie inside and reached into my pocket and grabbed a twenty-dollar bill.

"Hey, Louie, you ready to take down the house today?"

"Shit yeah brother, let's do it."

We decided to play one of the Florida tracks, Gulfstream Park. I had been an avid horse racing handicapper for some time and Louie was just as good. We made a very formidable team.

Louie was checking the eighth race on the card when he said, "Pete, this race is your specialty. It's a maiden race on the turf."

Maiden races are for two years old horses that haven't won or raced yet. The turf are races that are run on the grass. I knew the breeding of the horses and how well their sires and dams did on grass. I was able to tell if they had a good chance of winning their first time out. I also knew when trainers would hold their horses back the first time out.

Louie only liked one horse in the race. I was able to come up with the three other horses I felt would come in second and third when they crossed the finish line. We did a three-horse exacta box. That would be for first and second place for ten dollars. Then, we did a four-dollar triple box for first, second, and third.

The horses burst out of the gate. One of our horses went right into the lead. Down the stretch they went, and our lead horse won easy. Then, our second and third picks came right behind him.

We turned seventy-five dollars into six thousand dollars. I guess it wasn't a bad day after all. I think that was God's way of lending me a helping hand.

Whenever I had to report for parole it was always strange and grimy feeling for me. I waited in a room on the third floor at 100 Livingston Street in Brooklyn, NY. There were at least sixty parolees waiting to report to their respective parole officer.

Some were reporting for their first check in. Others were doing their weekly or monthly check in. Even out of prison, the hardcore convicts sized each other up. Some were more than likely looking for a partner to commit their next score with. Many convicts can't adapt to life outside. So, they commit crimes to be put back in. This I know to be one of the truest facts about being a number to the system.

My P.O called me into his office. "Pete, how are things going for you in terms of employment?"

"It's a slow grind to be honest. My record keeps screwing me up when it comes to getting a job in the investigation and security field."

"Let me make a few calls for you. Have you ever thought about being a fireman?"

"No, not really. I think I'm in good enough shape to pass the physical test, and I'm confident I can pass the written test."

"Let me call a friend of mine who is a captain in F.D. He might be able to make a few calls and slip you through the cracks and get you in. Then your city P.D time would also be applied.

You would be out in ten years with your pension."

"I appreciate all your help."

"Remember if you leave the state call me first for permission."

"Yes, sir I will."

The next month I showed up for my next appointment. I was called into my P. O's office again. "Sorry, Pete, no luck with the F.D. job."

"I kind of was expecting that. No problem, thanks for trying. I was thinking about going back into the fugitive recovery business. I still have my license."

"Pete, I would think twice about that. Any fuck ups and you'll be violated, and I won't be able to help you. What if one of your skips goes wrong and you have to use force? That could really become a problem for you. Look, I know you still feel like a cop inside, but the truth is, you aren't, my friend. I'm sorry to say that to you."

"I don't know how to do anything else sir."

"First things first, stop calling me sir, just call me Mack. Second, here is my cell number. You call if you need to talk anytime. You're still one of us as far as I'm concerned, Pete. See you next month. Kyour head up; it'll all work out."

A month later my good friend Pat called me and asked if I needed work. We were in the same company in the academy. "Yes, brother, I can start right away if you need me tonight."

"Okay be at Club the Tunnel in Manhattan, it's right off the West Side Highway Downtown. Wear all black, the shift starts at 9:00 p.m. and ends around 4:30 a.m."

It was a gig in a nightclub. The first shift I worked at was on a Sunday night–the famous Hip Hop night. I was in for a rude awakening to the type of security work I would be doing.

Hip Hop night at the Tunnel was extremely violent and dangerous. I arrived early, and as I approached the club there was a sea of men wearing all black. These guys were huge and looked like they were ready for a fucking war. I was happy to see several ex-cops who I had been in the academy with. Some of them had left the job on their own terms for personal reasons. Others were like me and had been terminated for not following the rules and guidelines of the department.

Pat came up to me and explained what my responsibilities would be for the night. "Brother, you'll be a roamer for tonight. You'll be inside in the club walking around." He then introduced me to my partner, Pete, whom I am still great friends with to this day.

The Tunnel wasn't like any regular club I had ever been in. It had shared bathrooms, VIP rooms where patrons drank Crystal and Hennessey. I could always smell the marijuana being smoked throughout the club. The club was loaded with drug dealers from Manhattan, Queens, Staten Island, the Bronx, Long Island, and New Jersey. At any time, something could jump off and erupt creating an all-out war. Most nights there was always an incident which would result in fists flying or shots being fired outside the club. That's why Pat had close to eighty men and women working the club's security. I was paid off the books at first, one hundred dollars a night. Later I was able to be put on the books and received a check each week. That helped me provide the proper paperwork to my parole office to show I was gainfully employed.

CHAPTER TWENTY-FOUR

The first two years after my incarceration, life was good to me. I was making good money on and off the books with my security details. My bosses, Pat, and Rob, took care of me by letting me work the front door and roaming inside the clubs I worked in. These clubs were all based in Manhattan. I worked the Tunnel, the Palladium, and the Kit Kat club. My partner and I always had each other's back any time shit went down in or outside the clubs.

Working in that type of environment was extremely dangerous, and I needed to stay out of trouble with the law. But inevitably, the club saw violence most nights.

Pete, Rob, and Pat made it a priority to keep me hidden in the shadows whenever the NYPD were called for an assault inside the club. They made sure that I wasn't around to be questioned by the cops. They didn't want me to get violated on my parole.

I had the privilege of working beside several men who were highly trained in many styles of Martial Arts. Some were trained in Karate, Judo, Jujitsu, and Aikido. They were men you wanted on your side when violence erupted in and out of the clubs.

One Sunday night during a hip-hop party at the Tunnel, Pat told me to work behind the bar. My assignment was to protect the bartenders and barmaids from unruly customers. The club had several bars upstairs and on the main dance floor. I was assigned to protect the main bar.

Every hour or two the bartenders would empty their overflowing cash registers. The money would be placed into a bag that had a zipper with a lock on it. Then twenty to thirty security guards would walk through the crowd in a straight line in what I called a wedge.

Their hands would be on the shoulders of the man in front them. That was done to protect the supervisor holding the main cash bag who was either Pat or Rob. They would be in the middle carrying hundreds of thousands of dollars. That was the only way to prevent someone from stealing the money.

It was around 1:30 a.m. and there was a young black man at the bar who was surrounded by four of his companions. I had figured it was a high-level drug dealer. The barmaid was extremely busy serving other patrons when I heard the man yell, "Can I have a bottle of Crystal?"

She replied, "Yes, give me a minute and I will get you your order."

About a minute later he yells, "Yo, it's way past a minute give me my bottle."

"Okay I'll be with you in a second."

"Hey, bitch give me the fucking Crystal now, you fucking cunt."

That's when I stepped in front of the barmaid and said "Hey bud, relax you can see how busy it is in here. Give her a break and be respectful."

"Who the fuck are you, asshole?"

"I'm the guy that says if you get served or if you don't, motherfucker."

The guy started to lean in toward me, and I gave him an opened handed mush to his face. Sending him backwards. In a split second three of his watchdogs jumped over the bar and were on me instantly. We started fighting, throwing fists and elbows. Behind the bar was tight and there wasn't much room to move. To be honest, I was getting my ass handed to me by those big bastards. Within a minute, my backup came, and they were ripping the guy's bodyguards to shreds.

Pat grabbed me and shouted, "Get into the office now."

Pete went with me and we waited for Pat and Rob to come in. Rob spoke first.

"Pete, do you know who you just open handed in the face?"

"No, I have no clue who that scumbag is."

"That is Puffy."

I turned to Pete and asked him, "Pete, what the fuck is a Puffy?"

The three of them started to crack up uncontrollably.

Pat said, "We grew up with him in the Bronx. He is a big-time record producer."

"Oh, okay cool, sorry I had no idea."

Later that night I went over and apologized, and he actually apologized to the barmaid. That was one funny night and there would be a lot more to come.

The hip-hop parties were the most profitable nights for me, but they were also the most dangerous events to work. The holiday season were the longest shifts and by far the craziest nights to work in any of the clubs.

New Year's Eve 1999, Pete and I were working in the Palladium, the main money maker for the Canadian who owned the three clubs. Ecstasy and cocaine were being sold throughout the club. People were having all types of sex in the stalls of the men's and women's rooms. If they weren't fucking or giving blow jobs, they were snorting coke and swallowing pills.

The club was packed that night it was mainly as a gay and lesbian event. That crowd could party all night and go right into the next afternoon.

Around 3:00 a.m. the singer Ol' Dirty Bastard (ODB) and the Wu-Tang Clan band came into the club for some late-night drinks and fun. The only problem was, they only came to the club that night for one reason, to start a massive brawl with the gay and lesbian crowd.

While Pete and I roamed the club waiting in the shadows of the people dancing, Ol' Dirty Bastard purposely lunged into a dancing man. After that, all hell broke loose. Fights erupted all over the dance floor. Pete and I went after the hip-hop band. Fists, kicks, and furniture were flying. Pete was brawling with the singer, and I had one of the Wu-Tang groupies. I smashed my forehead into the bridge of the guy's nose, and down he went like a ton of bricks. Joining Pete in the melee, the fight continued into the hallway next to the office. We kicked Ol' Dirty Bastard down the stairs with a bunch of his security people.

There was only one problem, the door that led to the stairway was locked. There had to be close to eight people down the stairs. Ol' Dirty Bastard was pissed because we had pummeled the living shit out of him.

He was screaming at Pete and I, "Word to my mother, I will kill you. Word is bond."

I asked my good man, Pete, "What the hell does word is bond mean?"

"Fuck if I know brother."

Pete grabbed the fire extinguisher off the wall, and I pumped it to max level.

As ODB continued yelling, "Word to my mother."

Pete unleashed the cannon of fire spray directly into ODB's face hitting his opened mouth. The spray hit him hard knocking him backwards into his entourage. Pete kept dousing the crowd to keep them at bay until our backup came to assist us. The fight ended a few minutes later and the Wu Tang Clan were escorted out of the building without further incident. Or so we had thought.

Around 7:00 a.m., I was standing out front of the Palladium with a few other bouncers when a Black Escalade was driving up Second Avenue at a snail's pace. One of the passengers in the rear of the truck yelled out, "Nobody fucks with the Wu-Tang Clan."

He then aimed a flare gun at me and the other bouncers and fired it at us. The fire ball headed in our direction but missed its mark hitting the top of the club's billboard.

Several of the guards who were carrying pulled out their firearms and went to fire back, but Pat yelled, "Put your pieces away, we don't need anyone getting locked up over this bullshit."

I can remember working outside the KitKat club on a cold winter night. I was wearing a Russian hat that had fur inside and around the outside of it. If it got cold, I'd unsnap the buttons on top and the ears flaps would fall and provide extra warmth to my head. Well, during the late hours a fight broke out inside the club and there had to be at least twelve people fighting. Patrons and bouncers were going fist to cuff. A large black male went to square off with me. I took an Aikido stance to wait for his attack then, I would use his force against him. We circled each other for a minute exchanging obscenity.

Finally, he said "Man, I can't fight nobody wearing a rabbit on his head." We shook hands and hugged each other while simultaneously laughing our asses off.

Working those clubs were some of the most chaotic times of my life. But I had no other choice at the time. I needed to make a living to help support my kids.

CHAPTER TWENTY-FIVE

In 2001, I was getting rejected from all the jobs I had been applying for. It began to take a toll on me. It was like I had heaven and hell battling over my soul. There was a point in my life where I had become good friends with a few made guys. I recounted my story to Frankie and Johnny when Frankie said, "Let me talk to my friend and see if he can help you out."

"Thank you, Frank, I appreciate that."

Several days later he called me and said, "Pete, meet me at 1:00 p.m. at the OTB parlor in Staten Island. It's on Victory Blvd."

"Sounds good bud, see you then."

The next afternoon I met Frankie who introduced me to an older gentleman named Joey. He was one of the Captains in the Bonanno family.

"Frankie tells me some good things about you. The main thing I like about you is your loyalty. So, tell me kid, did the cops offer you any deals to keep your job? Did that include you ratting on other cops to get the charges thrown out if you complied with them?"

"That is correct, Joey. I refused to give up any cops for their bullshit deal. I did my time and never did or would sellout any cops."

"Well Frankie's word is good for me kid. He's vouching for you. You'll help him out when he needs something done. Are you good with that? Frankie let's give him a new name. How about Berretta?"

"Sounds good to me, Joey."

Even with the kindness of Joey, times were still tough

when it came to finding a job on or off the books. I had to rely on my horse racing knowledge to make ends meet. The main problem with that, was, if I botched a few races and I'd be in the poorhouse for days. I didn't need my balls being broke by my kids' mother. I guess she had a right to get pissed when I couldn't find employment. Truth of the matter is, I should've never gone home after I'd been released. But I needed to be with my children to protect them.

I wasn't thinking like a cop like I had done the past fourteen years. Even though I knew I couldn't be a police officer and never would be again, I tried to be on the right side of the law. That was the only thing good left in me, knowing I still had some blue blood running through my veins.

Frankie had given me his football betting sheet and all the locations he controlled in Brooklyn. I would go all over to the local bars on Tuesdays giving the betting sheets out. For each betting sheet that someone placed I would make a half of dollar. On an average week I would make $500.

After the football season had finished Frankie called and said, "Pete, tomorrow meet us at the OTB in Staten Island at 2:00 p.m."

"Sounds good, see you then Frankie."

The next day the three of us sat in the far corner away from any prying ears. Joey said, "Okay Berretta, are you ready to step up to the big leagues and make some real money?"

"I want to hear what the job is first, Joey."

Joey laid out the plan to rob one of the nightclubs in Manhattan. He knew when and where the accountant would be making the clubs nightly deposit to a night drop box at the Chase bank.

"You'll be Frankie's eyes and ears for the job. If you feel the accountant is going to resist, knock her out and snatch the bag. There should be anywhere between fifty to one hundred thousand in the bags. Our split is seventy percent divided three ways. Are you in? The gig goes down next Saturday night, September 14."

"Joey, I need a day or two to mull this over."

"Don't think too hard Beretta."

Two days later I felt myself thinking like a criminal. If I went through with this heist, I would be a true criminal in the next few days. That is how desperate my life had become. I hated my life and the system. It had broken me at that time. The more I was broken, the more I evolved into a person that would commit crimes. Everything I stood for, all the good in me was being drained slowly and I was beginning to consider Joey's proposition.

September 11, 2001, would change the lives of Americans forever. It had transformed me back into a devote Roman Catholic. The war between good and evil within myself continued to have a grip on my body and soul.

What I am about to tell you is my own experiences with heaven and hell. Take it for what it is and decide for yourself. A few days after the bombing, I was feeling guilty that I couldn't be in the trenches with my blue brothers and sisters. I felt that I should be searching for people who may still be alive. It was killing me inside that so many cops and firemen had lost their lives trying to save the innocent victims of the terrorists. It tore me apart that I couldn't do anything to help them.

I went to bed that night and from what I can honestly tell you, I had an out of body experience or some sort of a heavenly dream. When laid on my futon, I fell asleep just like any normal night. Suddenly, awake I thought I had woken up from an intense nightmare. I was now above my body watching myself sleep.

That is when Mary, the mother of Jesus, touched my shoulder. She asked me, "Peter, you would never be my son's adversary, would you?"

At that moment I felt my true self come back. The blue blood returned within me and was once more pumping through my veins with fury. My eyes welled up, and I turned to Mary and answered. "I will never abandon your son or you Mary."

Then I fell back into my body and woke up sweating and crying. What the fuck just happened to me? Was that real, or a dream? I knew one thing for sure, I wouldn't be doing that job for Frankie and Joey. I called Frank in the morning and cut all ties with them for good.

Many months later I was still going through tough times. Evil was knocking on my door, but I wouldn't answer. So, I took a trip up to Pennsylvania to visit my mother.

Later in the evening, I went to bed and fell into a deep sleep. A black shadowy figure emerged over me. It was on top of me and spoke these words, "Let yourself go and come with me. You have been through enough and deserve to prosper. Come with me where you truly belong."

I knew damn well who and what it was. It was Lucifer. That's what I believe in my heart to this day.

"You're coming with me now."

I was frozen on the bed, his weight crushing me. At that moment, my soul was going to give into the dark lord. I had had enough suffering. The dark figure jammed its hand down onto my chest. His fingers had long claws, and they pressed into me with vengeance causing my body and soul to beg with relief. I felt the life inside me being draining–my lungs were going to burst.

Then, I remembered what a nun had told my mother when my father committed suicide. "God only gives tremendous suffering to those who can handle it. Because others cannot endure those personal trials. The lord chooses his toughest soldiers at birth to fight for others to give them hope."

That's when my hands were freed, and I yelled, "I will never abandon God. Never."

The dark figured vanished and seconds later I woke up. I was dripping in sweat and my chest was in terrible pain. I looked down at myself and there, upon my chest, I saw a large red spot. I was too afraid to go back to sleep and stayed up the rest of the night.

My last experience was a few days after one of my good childhood friends Nick had committed suicide. He was plagued with his own demons and felt that needed to leave this world. It bothered me immensely that I wasn't there for him when he had needed me most.

I kept thinking, "Why, couldn't I have saved him?" I asked God that question so many times I had lost count.

One night after Nick's death, I was sleeping in my den on the futon. I had been in a deep slumber possibly dreaming, I can't even remember. What I do remember is that when I opened my eyes, I was in hell.

The ground was made up of grey and deep red stone, and each one was deeply cracked. In between those cracks were little rivers of red and orange lava. The branches of the trees were bare and burnt, large thorns stuck out of the trunks and branches. There were various demon looking creators before me and they all looked like they were getting ready to tear me into pieces.

I ran as fast as I could, no direction in mind just away from there. Amidst my running, I saw two people that had been in my life. My father and my friend Nick.

I yelled to Nick, "Grab my hand Nicholas, I'll get you out of here."

He extended his sweaty shaking hand, and I gripped it as tight as I could. At that moment when I had grabbed Nick, I looked into my father's eyes just for split second before turning away from him.

"Let's go home, Nick. God forgives you for taking your life."

I woke up throwing my legs off the futon. Leaning over,

I ran my hands across my neck feeling the vast amount of perspiration that had accumulated. My body was on fire.

For some reason my tongue hit the roof of my mouth and I realized the inside was completely peeled off. I spit the dead skin into my hand. It was as if I had eaten a scorching piece of pizza and the hot cheese melted the roof of my mouth. But I knew I had had no hot meals that day or night.

I stayed awake the rest of the night very unnerved, but I was relieved that Nick was up in heaven where he belonged. These situations are ones I keep in my mind every day and believe saved me.

I remain a devout Roman Catholic and refuse to convert to the new ways of the church wanting to keep the old ways.

It feels good to be a part of the blue family again. I'll always be on the right side of the law. I have learned so many times in my life that only through pain can you achieve greatness. And I know that I have not yet achieved that. But I have survived everything that life has thrown at me. As many times as I get knocked down, I will keep getting back up. Things always happen for a reason.

CHAPTER TWENTY-SIX

While I was working at the clubs, the Division of Alcoholic Beverage Control and the NYPD started cracking down on the underage drinking in all the nightclubs in the city. The other problem was there were so many fights in the clubs that the DOJ (Department of Justice) came down with a new ordinance. All security personnel needed to be licensed.

This presented me with a new problem. There would be no way that I could legally obtain a security license in the state of New York. I would have to get paid off the books. The owner of the clubs didn't want any type of legal problems. So, I was let go and needed to find a loophole in the restrictions or get what is known as a certificate of relief. That would enable me to be employed on the books. That document basically sweeps a nonviolent offender's record under the rug in most instances.

I completed all the necessary paperwork and mailed it into the proper channels. It took six months to receive the state's decision, which of course, was a denial. Judge Allen had refused to sign off on the paperwork.

In 2001 my family and I moved from Brooklyn to Long Island. I wanted my children to be involved in sports and get a better education in the public schools on the Island. I started coaching my kids in several sports: softball, baseball, football, and wrestling.

While I was coaching my son's baseball team, I had formed a friendship with a man named Joe who owned a security and investigation company. After a few weeks, I felt comfortable telling him my story and my background. He welcomed me with open arms into the company. I'd be working under the company's umbrella as an investigator which entitled me to do security for them under the roll of consultant.

I'd become one of the BSI's best investigators. They had many retired cops and corrections officers working for them during the 2000's. I had been one of the only investigators that would go into the city without a firearm and still do an investigation without being nervous. Joe knew I had extensive knowledge of the streets in Brooklyn, Queens, and Manhattan. My stronghold being Harlem and Washington Heights which is Uptown Manhattan. So, when a case was up in that area, I usually went with one of the bosses to sit on the subject and videotape them. It was where I was at home and at my best when it came to being an investigator.

During the year 2006 Joe called me into the office and said, "We have a job for you, but it's dangerous. There is a chance that if you get made while your videoing, you could be snatched up yourself. We are investigating a high-profile woman who happens to be married to a governor. He thinks she's sleeping around on him. She has Secret Service agents guarding her from her end of the family, and he has the Secret Service on his end. So, there will be several government agents to contend with. If you're caught shooting pictures or videoing taping, there is a chance, they'll grab you. If that happens more than likely, you'll be taken to an undisclosed area and questioned. Possibly roughed up to get a confession out of you as why you're shooting video on their asset. If this happens Pete, you'll be on your own. There can be no backlash to our client. Are you in or out for this assignment?"

"What is the pay for the job, Joe?"

"Thirty-five dollars an hour."

"I'm in, boss." My thought process at the time was "This is like a cloak and dagger investigation it could be action packed adventure."

I left for Midtown Manhattan later that afternoon with my recon gear. I made sure to wear all black and to keep me hidden in the shadows during nightfall. The subject was scheduled to do a book signing the next day.

I decided to take a stroll by the hotel she was staying at. There were Secret Service agents dressed as bellhops and doormen. I could easily see the earpieces they were wearing that were connected to their walkie talkies. There had been ten agents out in the front of the posh hotel, that was an issue. I couldn't just walk in and start filming her with the boyfriend.

I looked over the four corners of Lexington Avenue and decided to take photos from the Northside corner of Lex and 52nd Street. I was able to get a few snapshots of her coming out of the hotel and getting into a white Escalade. When I let the camera down, I knew I was in a shit load of trouble.

There were several agents walking towards me. Luckily for me there was a deli to my left that I was able to run into. Bolting through the deli I was to use the rear exit which people used to get to the other side of the next street. I jetted to 53rd and escaped down 3rd Avenue.

Waiting an hour for things to die down, I went back up 53rd and saw a church that extended from 52nd and 53rd. I decided to walk into the cathedral to pray and hopefully speak with one of the clergies.

I looked around for several minutes and saw that one of windows would give me a great view of the hotel. I knocked on the rectory door and I.D.-ed myself as an investigator. A friendly priest that was a cop-buff allowed me to do my surveillance in the church the whole night.

Around 6:00 a.m., the white Escalade pulled up to the hotel. The subject came out with another woman which I found kind of peculiar. When the other woman got into the SUV, she took off her wig. It was the guy the subject was sleeping with. I was able to get clear and precise photos and a short video of the two love birds meeting. It turned out that the wife was sleeping with our client's campaign manager.

A few months later, we started to do a lot of workers

compensation cases for a big airline company. Whenever I did those cases for Joe, I had a steady partner. His name was Al, and he was a retired corrections captain. Al and Joe held the same rank and worked together for many years. They both had seen their share of action while they were in law enforcement. We would videotape men and women cheating the airline pretending to be out injured or on sick leave. The scam artists were collecting a nice paycheck. That is, until we came into the picture and exposed them for insurance fraud.

There were times I would pretend to be injured and would be waiting in the same waiting room at a doctor's office. I would be sitting right across from the people who were scamming the airline. I would get him or her on video inside the doctor's office feigning an injury. Inevitably the subject would leave the doctor's office and as soon as they were out of sight, their bad back or leg was miraculously cured. We helped close a ton of fraudulent cases for the airline.

While working for BSI I had worked on two important cases with Joe's investigation company. I was one of the lead investigators on both. The first case started out in Manhattan.

The targets were a group of employees who worked for a graphic design company. The company was in a bidding war with several other agencies to create a new logo for the Wrigley 5 gum. They'd hit their mark with a great graphic design and planned to unveil it to Wrigley's.

There was just one problem. A group of their employees led by a woman from Connecticut stole the artwork and the companies pitch to close the multimillion-dollar deal. The lead woman had recruited several other employees to help her get the designs out of the building. I followed the three main players involved in the heist of the graphic designs.

I was following them twelve hours a day for a week straight. My assignment was to follow the briefcase where the plans were being kept in. I pursued the ringleader on foot in the streets of Manhattan for several days. Then, tailed her on the subway where she finally handed the briefcase off to her second in charge. He proved to be the hardest to track. He was overly cautious and showed signs of knowing he was being tailed. I decided to tell Joe, and he made the decision to have myself and two other investigators leapfrog the man. One of us would follow for a block or two, and fall off, then another guy would take up his position. I carried several different clothes to wear while pursuing the subject. He really gave us a run for our money.

We tailed that bastard for two days through three states; New York, New Jersey, and Connecticut. He was on foot, in taxis, and in trains. The briefcase never left his person.

Midweek, he finally handed the merchandise to another male who immediately took the case into a building in Midtown Manhattan. That Friday, I was given 20 subpoenas to serve to the ex-employees. They had opened a corporation and set up shop in a building in Midtown. My main problem was I had no idea what floor or office they were in. We were running out of time to serve the subpoenas. I only had a little window of time left to get the job done.

Joe called me into the office and said, "Pete, we have until midnight to get these documents served to all twenty people. Take Ramos with you and get the job done. We need this one."

"Ten-four, I won't let you down boss."

Ramos and I were in Manhattan by 6:00 a.m. that Friday. By 10:00 a.m., I had downed three cups of coffee and was so on edge I didn't even get out to take a piss. I had observed all twenty subjects entering the building, but I still had no clue what floor their office was on.

Then I got lucky, the security guard who worked the front desk came over to my car. She was a heavy-set black woman. May I add, she must have been a real catch in her hay days. The guard walked up to my car and motioned for me to roll my window down.

"Hi sugar, I have to ask you to move your car. You're

in one of our tenants parking spaces." I tinned her with my investigator's shield.

"l need, to see your identification, honey."

I showed her my I.D and replied, "I am so sorry, pretty lady, but I can't do that."

"Why the hell not, mister?"

"Well, can you keep a secret officer?"

"I sure can, sugar."

"We are investigating a group of people in your building."

"Shit big boy, you must be talking about that new group that just rented the office on the fourth floor."

"Fuck yeah I'm talking about them."

"Well, it's no skin off my bones. They're up in office 409. I don't like any of them. They're all rude to me, so screw them."

"Thank you dear, you're an angel."

I told Ramos to stay in the car until I gained entrance to the office. I took the elevator up to the fourth floor and stayed hidden at the end of the hallway behind the corner. Their office door was next to the men's room. I waited for one of their male employees to enter the bathroom. I was holding a folder that had the twenty subpoenas in it.

At 1:00 p.m. one of the employees went into the men's room. I quickly followed him in. I pretended to take a pee in a stall that wasn't close to him. Once he was through washing his hands and exited the bathroom, I held the handle of the bathroom door and waited until I heard the office door open. I made a dash to their door and was on him and inside the office in less than twenty seconds.

"Hello everybody, my name is Investigator Thron, I'm here to serve twenty of your employees subpoenas. When I call your name come up here and read the paperwork that has your name on it. Please be nice and sign on the dotted line."

Within a few minutes the group began getting angry and wanted to know why they were being served. I radioed to Ramos, "Hey, get up here I have ten people screaming in my face."

After an hour I had been able to serve all the employees and get all the paperwork completed. Days later they all became defendants and had to appear in criminal court. They were all charged with and indicted for corporate espionage and conspiracy.

The second case was another cloak and dagger mission. A very influential actress was being stalked. The perpetrator was of Middle Eastern descent. He had fallen in love with her and was sending her love letters every day. When he didn't receive a reply, he decided to take matters into his own hands. He boarded a plane and traveled to New York City.

On his first day in the Big Apple, he went right over to her apartment in the downtown area. The building had a doorman, and every visitor needed to be buzzed in. The subject had purchased three dozen roses and requested to be let into the building.

"Please sir, I need to speak with Carol, these roses are for her. I came a long way to confess my love for her."

The doorman held up his first finger and mouthed, "One second sir, I will let her know you are downstairs."

What the stalker didn't know was that Carol had hired Joe's investigation company.

"Sorry sir but she isn't home right now. You can leave the roses at the front desk. When Carol arrives, I will give them to her. Is that good for you?"

"I guess I have no choice. Here take these and tell Carol I said thanks a lot. I will be back every day with a new bouquet of flowers for her."

Later that afternoon we had a squad of six investigators who would be providing Carol protection 24-7. I took the midnight shift. I wanted to nail that sick bastard.

The second day I was working with Al. The stalker showed up at the building with another bouquet of roses. Al jumped out of the car and blocked the front entrance, "Sorry the building is closed to all visitors for the rest of the next week."

"That is total bullshit, I want to speak with Carol now."

Earlier I had given Al a gift, a new ASP which is a telescope expanding steel baton. He loved when I would snap it out whenever we were involved in an altercation. Al shot the ASP out and pressed it against the guy's chest.

"Take a walk buddy."

"You have no idea who you are fucking with. I will get Carol to fall in love with me no matter what I have to do."

I spoke into my walkie talkie. "Al let him go for now. I'll tail this prick on foot and see where and what he does throughout the day."

"Your call, brother."

"You get the fuck out of here and don't come back. She isn't interested in you. Leave her alone."

I let the guy get a few hundred feet away from our recon vehicle then hit the streets. That crazy SOB took me all the way to the West-Side Highway right into Hell's Kitchen. He had no idea he was venturing into the Irish mob's territory. He would stop into every Kinkos and make photocopies of some documents he had in his backpack. Al was never far behind ghosting me the whole time.

"Pete, what the hell is this crazy freak doing in in the photocopy stores?"

"Al, I have no idea. I'll follow him into the next one. Meet me at whatever corner I end up on and throw me my baseball cap and a different colored tee shirt."

"That is a big 10-4, brother."

I continued tailing the stalker for another ten blocks when he finally made it to his last Kinkos stop. I waited a few minutes and then entered the store. I walked to a copy machine on the other end of the aisle he was in. I walked by him as he was neatly putting his copies in a pile.

"Al, we have a big problem here. This crazy fucker must have two hundred copies of our client headshot photo. Get this brother, they're all the same picture. Call Joe and update him on what we have."

Our bad guy left the store quickly. He knew where his next destination was, and he was in a hurry to get there. I walked by our car and Al tossed me another baseball cap and new blue tee shirt.

I gave a quick time check and radioed Al, "Okay bud it's 2:15 p.m. he's moving fast and keeps checking his watch. Maybe he has to meet someone that's providing him with the information on our client."

At 2:50 he made his way into the West-Side Highway Park. "Al, are you seeing this brother? You're taping all of this, right?"

"Yes, indeed my friend, the video is rolling."

To be honest, I don't think the perp knew what part of the city he was in. That Park was famous for a lot of prostitute's, men, women, and transgender's looking to solicit horny patrons that wanted a quickie. As I walked through the park, I immediately felt dirty. All types of prostitutes were approaching me.

I just kept saying, "Not interested, please step aside."

Finally, halfway into the park, I see our guy take out a white mat from his backpack. He then grabbed our client's photo and placed it on the mat. He was doing his afternoon prayers along with worshiping the photo of his make-believe girlfriend.

"Al, inform the boss this sick fuck is praying to her picture."

The stalker presented a huge problem, and we felt he was extremely dangerous and posed a threat to her. We had no idea who his contacts were in the states or if he had any military training. Joe called his federal contacts who in turned informed the Israeli police. The next day the, Israeli's were in the states and snatched him up and put him on a flight to an unknown location. I'm thinking it was a black site and he would be getting questioned for a long time.

I was able to work with Joe until 2015. I learned a lot from him when it came to private investigations. I'll always be grateful to him for giving me the work and never doubting that I was screwed over by the system.

He always treated me as an ex-cop and once said to me, "Pete, you should look into getting a lawyer and see if you can get your case overturned."

My response was, "Joe, I could never put my family through that ordeal again."

Thinking back maybe I should have listened to him.

CHAPTER TWENTY-SEVEN

Twenty plus years has passed since my incarceration. When I was an inmate, it never registered in my mind that my family was doing their own type of prison sentence along with me, just on the outside. It took me until writing this book to ask them what they had gone through while I was in prison.

I have already explained the toll it took on my mother in my first book End of Tour. But hearing how it affected my brother and sister was heartbreaking. I also asked my future wife her thoughts about my past. She never once judged me or looked at me as a convict. In her eyes, I will always be an ex-cop.

You never realize the true depth or meaning of the word family until shit gets bad. Having an older sister who was much shorter than me was always a fun thing for me. Here I was the "baby" brother, and I towered over my "big" sister. She always looked out for me when I was kid, showing up to all my ballgames and my wrestling matches which I knew she hated watching because she always worried someone would hurt me. No matter what I always knew she would be somewhere in the stands and if I didn't see her, believe me when I say I could hear her.

My sister, along with my mother and brother, was proud of me when I was going to college on a baseball scholarship. She had more faith in me than anyone. But when things didn't pan out, I was devastated to have to tell her. I can still remember the look on her face–her heart broke for me.

There was nothing I could do so it was then that I made the decision to become a brother in blue. Telling my mom and older brother was bad enough, but telling my sister was a whole other situation. She was upset to say the least.

When I told her of my new career, it was a tough thing to do being that she was out of state. We would talk about Manhattan and how she loved to go shopping there, but the city was more than that for me. I loved it for its action.

My sister had two high school friends that had become cops and she always thought the profession was dangerous.

"Your fucking kidding me, right? Please tell me this is a cruel joke. You'll be carrying a gun, are you out of your mind?"

She was hurt, and she was mad and most of all she was terrified. I wasn't certain of anything at this time in my life. I was excited, maybe too much, and honestly wasn't thinking about anyone or anything else other than becoming a cop–it consumed me every minute of every day.

I watched a lot of cop movies and read various cop related books, and at night I prepared for the test. Now that I look back, I can tell you with 100% certainty, becoming a cop hurt my relationship with my sister. I would've never thought that would happen, but it also bonded us in ways that, until the writing of this book, I wasn't able to understand or appreciate.

When I write that I was obsessed with becoming a NYC cop, it's an understatement.

My sister got married in October of 1987 and I was in the midst of studying at the academy. She was the first of our family and our cousins to get married. So, her wedding was a big deal to say the least. It was held in Pennsylvania, and we had to drive several hours from New York to get to the hotel.

When I got there, I found my sister and without hesitation said to her, "Hey, I'm going to the church, but I can't stay for the entire reception. I have to study."

She shot me a look and said, "But our whole family is here, don't you want to spend time with them?" Mind you, this is the day before her wedding.

I looked down at her and told her, "I can't sis, I almost wasn't going to come. I have to study for three subjects, this is important to me. You don't understand how important this is." After that came out of my mouth, she stood there with a dumbfounded look on her face.

"Well, everyone will want to see you. I hope you can stay for a little while at least." With that she turned and walked away. Her words dripped with disappointment. I never wanted to disappoint my sister, and unfortunately, it wouldn't be the last time.

When you are in jail all you have is time–countless hours. Time to relive every conversation, every holiday, every family party, everything your mind can think of. I made sure I relived all the moments I had with my family because it took up time and I wanted to feel their love in any way I could.

Thinking about my life allowed me to feel other emotions. I thought about my sister's wedding. I remembered what she said, and I realized that even before her big day, she was thinking about others. She was thinking about me. I honestly think my sister thought I was going to get killed in the line of duty and she wanted me to make as many memories as I could before it happened.

She knew I could be reckless at times. Deep down, she also knew I wanted to protect my family and be the best at what I did when it came to being a cop. Sisters are funny creatures, they are emotional, caring and man are they judgmental.

I couldn't be there when she had her first born because I had been working a big case. And it wasn't the only time I missed my sister's accomplishments. My sister is a social worker and when I was first sent to jail, she was graduating with her BSW. In 1998, she graduated with my mother, brother, sister-in-law, and daughter in the audience. All I could do was sit in my dark jail cell trying to picture what she looked like in her cap and gown walking from Fordham to Lincoln Center.

I made excuses for fucking things up. First, I made it seem like I had no choice. Of course, that is what it feels like, but in the end everything we do is a choice. When I was working as a cop, I was either studying, working a case or I was testifying at court. Then, my excuse became jail after my incarceration.

I remember my sister had a horrible situation that took place on the bus ride from Pennsylvania to New York. Every Saturday, she rode the Greyhound to get to school. What I didn't know was that one day she got on the bus and was so tired she fell asleep in the back seat. When she woke up some skell, that she of course befriended earlier, was touching her while he was jerking off. She told me that she was frozen in fear and didn't move–just prayed that it'd soon be over.

When it was, he went into the bathroom and cleaned up. As he exited the bathroom, he walked to the front of the bus for the rest of the ride to New York.

All I could think about was that she had to call my brother. I should've been with my brother to help her at that time. After all I was the cop. I wasn't there to protect her. The motherfucker touched my sister!

This tiny little spitfire of a woman was reduced to fear, and I did nothing because I couldn't, my hands were tied. There are no words to write down on paper how I felt when she finally told me that story. The worst part of the whole thing was I could see in her eyes how much pain she was in and how a decade later it still affected her.

After she finished telling me, she finally said, "Pete, think about it, it's probably a good thing you were in jail because if you weren't incarcerated you would have ridden the bus with me until you found him and then you would have killed him."

My sister spent most of her career caring for the elderly and in doing that she learned a great deal about benefits, not just for her clientele, but for others.

It was always good when my family got together at the holidays and no matter what was going on in my life, the three of us always had a mutual respect for each other's paths. We were so far apart in personalities and our likes and dislikes but no matter what or when we were together, we were like glue. We loved hanging out, and we made each other laugh, but that wouldn't come for many years after I got out of jail.

The years following prison, my sister would regularly call and ask me about jobs and how things were going. Truthfully, as much as I loved my family it was hard for me to accept what I was and what I wasn't anymore. The years went by slow, however, as I look back now, it is hard to believe that I'm 22 years' post-prison.

I tried to keep the struggles with getting a job on the books from my family. Unfortunately, I had hit a wall that forced me to need assistance through programs run by the state.

During the year 2019, my mother broke her left hip. She had spent several months in rehab. My mother wanted out of there in the worst of ways. We took her home against our better discretion.

After six days, we received the call that she had fallen and had broken her other hip. She even caught the horrible Covid-19. That still didn't stop her, she has the heart of a lion and never stops fighting. Now she is living Upstate New York with family. After my mother got sick and everything had to be handled, my siblings and I began to talk to each other almost every day.\

I'm not one to just sit around and take money from the state for doing nothing, so once again as I had done a hundred times before, I set off to find a job. I wanted in the worst way to get back into the investigations field.

My thought process was, it's been over 20 years since prison, maybe I won't be looked at like a convict. Or worse, an ex-cop who became an ex-convict.

I'd once been told your record doesn't show up on criminal searches after ten years. Unfortunately, that information was wrong. The truth is, there is not much work for guys like me when companies check my background. All they see is that I became a criminal, not that I was once a cop. It infuriated the hell out of me knowing that I'm probably more qualified for the investigator position I'd applied for, than most of the other applicants.

Instead, men like me get out and aren't integrated back into the community. We're looked down upon without employers or people even knowing who we are. Subsequently, we're automatically judged without hesitation.

I'm very much like my sister. She has a need to help others and gives her all. My family has always said that some people go to school to become who they are. I realize now that I followed in my sister's footsteps. She was born to be a social worker, and I was born to be a cop.

Occasionally, I close my eyes and wonder where I would have been if the whole debacle in my life never happened. If I had been proven innocent of all the charges and went on to become a detective.

Throughout the past two years with all that has happened to my family, the great thing is the bond I have developed with my sister and brother.

We are taught that prison and jail are there to keep the bad guys in and rehabilitate the ones that can and want to be rehabilitated in order to pay their debt to society. This is to help them become a fully functioning member of society so that they can provide for their family and make their wrongs right.

One would think with this mindset, it wouldn't be so hard for guys like me to find employment and begin my life again. But in the end, with all that, I tried a hundred plus applications and walk-in interviews only to be denied or ignored.

My brother and I sat down one night, and he started to

tell me his feelings when I was in jail. He said, "I felt a sense of despair that ran deeper than I could completely trace. It left me empty and unmoored. The feeling of impotence at not being able to help was overwhelming. Before and during the initial months of your incarceration, I tried to find any way I could to help, to affect the situation in any way I could, but was completely unable to change the outcome. I even had a friend who said he was owed a significant favor from a very well-connected person, who we would normally not be connected to but who would be likely to have some influence, and said if I wanted, he would give me that favor. This would have put me in his debt, but it felt that if ever it was worth it, this would be the time. This person reached out and after a few days I was told that 'Someone really wants him to stay in jail and there's nothing to be done'. I felt like there was simply no way to help my brother at this point. I felt a sense of injustice that I was not able to reconcile.

"When you were released. I could barely contain the joy I felt. I wanted to monopolize my time but realized it was most important that I spend as much time with my family as possible."

He felt a relief that was physically palpable. Yet the world still seemed tilted slightly, off-axis, and he feared that it could tilt completely again at any moment with all that was going on around us in our great country.

I had met my fiancée on a dating site. We spoke through text messages and on the phone to get to know each other. She is a beautiful Asian woman, and she speaks fluent Russian and English.

On our first date, she said," Pete, I have to tell you the truth about something."

She went on to tell me her story, tell me all about her life and sole. After hearing her amazing story, I knew she was my soulmate. I then told her all about my past life.

I was so scared that she wouldn't want anything to do with a cop who went to prison. But that isn't what happened.

She looked into my eyes and said, "I know and can feel you are a good man and have a good heart."

I fell in love with her instantly and now she is part of my family as I am part of hers. That night, she welcomed me with open arms and never one has ever judged me for what had happened. For that, I want to thank my fiancée Adriana, my sister Janice, and brother Phil, for all their support and encouragement. They are the reason I keep moving forward in life and keep writing.

My three children really don't remember much of the past events that took me away from them for two years. They know what happened to me and they know some of my war stories as a cop. I tried to shield them from the horrors of jail.

I'm grateful that none of them has ever looked down on me for being an ex-con. I was blessed to have them in my life. I will always cherish watching them grow up and become respectful and hardworking adults in society.

CHAPTER TWENTY-EIGHT

I have worked in many professions after my incarceration–most were off the books. I worked on elevators installing the new cabs for people to ride in. That was one of the most dangerous and poor choice of job I have ever done. I installed thousands of data cables for IBM in the NYC schools. I was a decent carpenter. In 2006, I worked construction, and I witnessed my boss fall from a second story floor of a house and break his forearm in half, fracture his jaw and skull. That was the last time I ever swung a hammer for anyone other than my family or myself.

That same year, I coached my son's football team. I noticed another coach speaking to clients on three separate cell phones. I took a few steps closer and heard him talking about professional and college football. I decided to ask Willey what he did for a living.

"I am a sports handicapper."

"What the hell is that?"

"Have you ever seen Two for The Money? It stars Al Pacino and Matthew McConaughey, they play sports handicappers. Pacino is the boss, and he has a bunch of guys selling sports picks. Hey, you are knowledgeable when it comes to football. Why don't you come by the office tomorrow night, around 6:00? I'll show you what I do and introduce you to my boss?"

"Sounds good, I'm between jobs anyway."

The next day I was in Willey's office and listening to how he pitched his clients, for tens of thousands of dollars. They were paying him for his expertise and advice on college football. He was what gamblers consider a betting sharp.

For the next nine years, I worked for that company giving out sports picks. In this type of profession, most guys will use a fictitious name–including myself. The main reason for that is gamblers hate to lose. So, if a client pays a handicapper for information and that information falls through, you have one very upset gambler who may threaten to kill you.

I started to work for myself in 2015 selling sports information. The problem is that there are so many people doing it now, that sometimes it can be a dead-end career path. The industry is flooded with wannabes that sell picks for a dollar or five dollars. I still sell picks to my steady clients because I'm fortunate enough to have a few guys that have stuck with me for several years. The reason for that loyalty is I really study the games and try to come up with the most accurate information possible. I always try to give them a betting edge over their book.

At one point in 2015, I had a very productive year for my clients, as well for myself. I also became an above average "Texas Hold 'em" player. I did the WPT or World Poker Tour circuit in Atlantic City and ended up cashing in at five events. My total winnings were close to twenty-five thousand dollars. I became a ranked poker player and horse racing handicapper for a little while.

When I met my fiancée in 2018, I had decided to throw my hat back into the investigation ring. My thinking was, "It has been over twenty years since I was incarcerated. What the hell do I have to lose."

Nothing was on my record besides me being a nonviolent offender. I put in for several investigator jobs. Nothing was happening–no call backs. Zilch. That is until the summer of 2019, when I was called back by the NYC Legal Aid Society. I was ecstatic to learn I had been selected to be interviewed.

July 15, 2019, I was called into the Queens Public Defenders office. I sat down at a long oval table. The head of the unit was on my right and next to her were two defense attorneys. On my left were three investigators. The one sitting next to me was the head of the investigator's unit. The boss of the attorneys advised me that myself and two retired NYPD detectives had been selected out of hundred and fifty applicants for the last two open positions. So, the whole time I was thinking, I must have passed their background check. Otherwise, why would they have call me into be interviewed?

After answering a mountain of their questions, the boss said to me, "Pete, I have one last question for you. How will you feel if you're on call one night and I tell you that we must defend a child rapist? How will you go about doing that investigation?"

Shit, she had to ask me something like that. That crime is a subject I hold dear to my heart. Child abusers and sexual abusers are the scum of the earth. Those are the worst predators. How do I answer that fucked up question and still have a chance of getting this job?

I took a deep breath and tried to slow my heartbeat down. At that moment, I felt like I was on a rooftop getting ready to swoop down on a drug dealer again. "Well, I would do the most thorough investigation as I possibly could. I would try to ensure that the defendant received a fair trial. I would try to gather as much evidence to assist the attorneys to properly defend their client."

The head investigator spoke first. "Pete, that was by the far the most articulate answer anyone has said during these interviews. Well, done, sir. None of us at this table condone that type of criminal act. We all feel they should rot in jail, but we have a job to do and we do the best we can for these mutts."

He looked around the table at the others and said, "He is our guy. Let's get him before another office tries to snatch him up."

I left the office confident that the job was mine. A few days later I received the call. "Pete, can you start this September?"

"Yes, thank you for the opportunity."

"Okay the main office in Manhattan will be in touch with

you to get all your personal information."

A day later the Manhattan office called and said, "We will be sending you all the paperwork to fill out for the title of Investigator. Please complete it as soon as possible and mail it back to us. It takes some time to get you into the system."

That Friday the packet came in the mail and on the last page I had to fill out was the background check. One of the questions was the one I always dreaded.

Have you ever been convicted of a crime? If you have, that will not disqualify you when it pertains to obtaining the position you are applying for. If you have been convicted of a felony, please explain the reason and what led to these circumstances.

Well, that's exactly what I did–in very articulate detail and to the point. I explained how the judges who presided over my hearings and trial were biased against any law enforcement personnel. The first was Judge Andrews who had ruled on the Map and Wade hearings and ruled in favor of the state. I explained that he didn't want to try my case because he was moving up to the appellant court. So, he passed it onto Judge Allen.

That same judge ended up being one of the six judges who presided over my appeals case and refused to recuse himself. That, in itself, was a blatant form of corruption. Did the rest of the appellant judges think he would rule against his own findings? Of course, not. That is because it would have opened a huge lawsuit against the city. They would've had to give me my job back or had me retire at the rank of detective. The city would have had to reimburse me all that back pay, and the state would have had to compensate me for the two years I was imprisoned.

That's basically what I wrote in my letter, and I went on further to explain to the head of the department that I would be an essential asset to them. I had extensive knowledge of being on both sides of the law.

Weeks went by and I heard nothing. To me, that was a good sign. So, my fiancée and I decided to buy me a professional wardrobe for my new job. The day before I was to report for work, I received an email from the Queens Legal Aid Society.

"We regret to inform you that we cannot hire you. We feel it would be a conflict of interest to the Public Defender's office and the defendants we are representing. We reached out to Judge Andrews, and he advised us not to hire you. The main reason is if you had to testify at trial on our client's behalf, we feel that your past record and the charges of falsifying business records would come into play. We wish you success in your endeavors."

Fuck you very much.

What really disturbed my family was the lack of disrespect they had when it came to the timing of the email. Not even a phone call to let me know of their decision. They hid behind their desk and simply hit the send button. Then they had the audacity to reach out to the corrupt judge who wouldn't recuse himself on my appeal.

To this day, I still cannot get a handle of how deep the corruption is in the city of New York runs. It has been well over twenty years since I was incarcerated, and I'm still paying for it.

After the disappointing new, I decided to get my personal trainer's license. I figured I might as well get paid to do something I loved.

I took the test and passed it easily. Then I got recertified for my CPR training. I applied to several gyms that summer. First, I was called by La. Fitness, NYCHC, then Planet Fitness, and finally Blink fitness. Each one of them had informed me that the position was mine if I wanted it. Of course, I wanted to work in any gym.

During the interviews I even went the extra mile by being honest and telling them about my history. Well needless to say, even after being guaranteed the job, the second I divulged the information of my past, I never received a call back to report for work.

My conviction has even so much as prevented me from getting social security disability from injuries I received while performing my duties as a police officer.

This book was not written out of self-pity. It is to make the readers aware of the horrors of jail and the repercussions that myself and other nonviolent offenders can suffer after they are released.

The question to ask yourself and the answer I need to know is, "How do I pay back to society when society will not allow me to pay it back?"

More to come.

THE END

About the Author

Pete Thron was born and raised in Long Island, New York. He was a New York City Housing police officer for nearly a decade during the era of crack cocaine. During his time as a cop, he encountered some of the most violent and deadly drug organizations in New York City. He personally made over 600 arrests and assisted in over a thousand others. He was awarded over 100 medals and written commendations for bravery and successful convictions of violent offenders. He also worked as an investigator and fugitive recovery agent for nearly a decade. He has three children and is a grandparent. He currently works as a sports consultant and is the author of the End of Tour series.

Made in the USA
Middletown, DE
24 March 2022